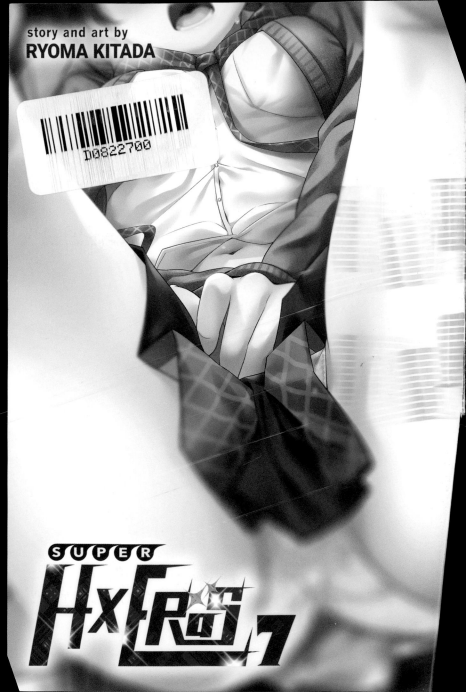

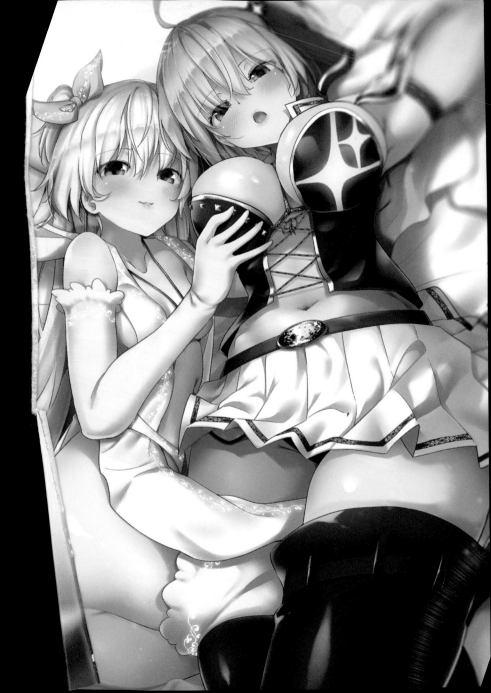

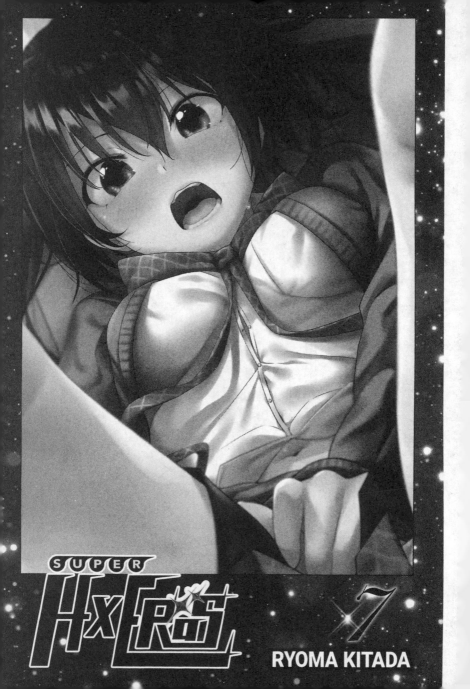

HXEROS Characters

HXEROS: A team of heroes that use the power of eros and H-Energy to fight the alien Kiseichuu.

Maihime Shirayuki
HXE White

A sweet, clumsy girl who looks normal on the outside but is a total horndog on the inside.

Momoka Momozono
HXE Pink

Tired of always being in her sister's shadow, she took up the superhero mantle. Has caught onto Retto's feelings for Kirara.

Kirara Hoshino
HXE Yellow

Extremely averse to sex and sexual innuendo due to a traumatic attack in her youth. Haunted by a hallucination of her younger self: Dark Kirara.

Retto Enjo
HXE Red

Became a hero to avenge his child-hood friend, Kirara, after a Kiseichuu attack traumatized her as a child. Coincidentally, also in love with her.

Story

The Earth as we know it is in peril: The horrifying Kiseichuu have come to destroy the human race! Thankfully, a team of young men and women have risen to the challenge to fight them off, day in and day out. Their name? The SUPER HXEROS.

When the HXEROS squad is forced to disband, Retto begins to fight Kiseichuu on his own in secret—that is, until his uncle is arrested by rules put into place by the new governor. After some investigating, the team finds out that this new governor is none other than the Kiseichuu Queen and engage her in an epic battle! Right at the end, though, a girl in a black HXEROS outfit shows up to confront them?!

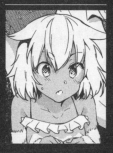

Chacha

Shunned Kiseichuu Princess. Has the ability to amplify H-Energy.

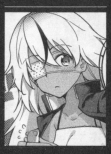

Murasame Shiko

Member of the Tokyo Squad. Wants to make Retto her benefriend.

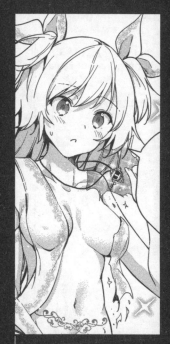

Sora Tenkuji

HXE Blue

Loves to draw hentai manga. In charge of designing the XERO Suits.

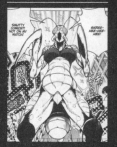

Kiseichuu

Evil aliens who seek to destroy humanity by draining their H-Energy, the source of human sexual desire.

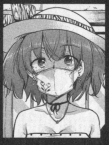

Wakakusa Moena

Member of the Tokyo Squad. Went to Momoka's middle school.

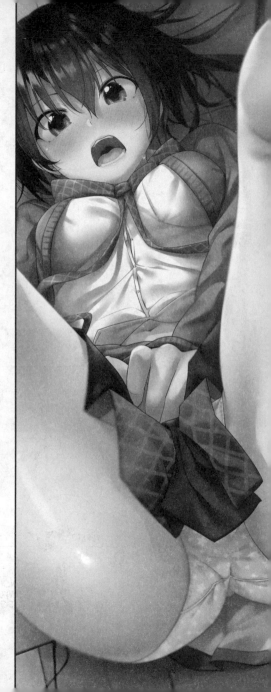

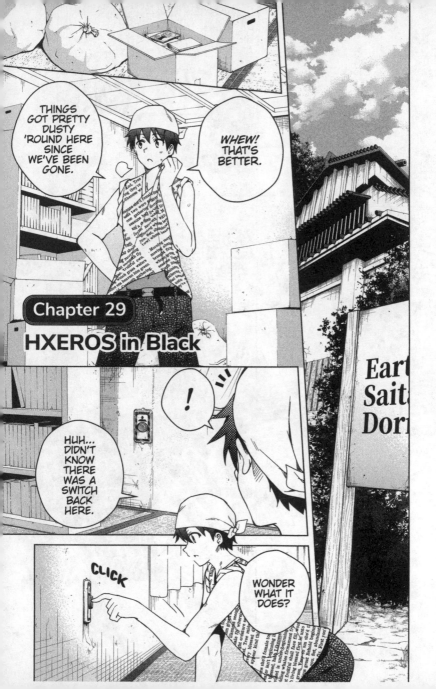

THINGS GOT PRETTY DUSTY 'ROUND HERE SINCE WE'VE BEEN GONE.

WHEW! THAT'S BETTER.

Chapter 29

HXEROS in Black

!

HUH... DIDN'T KNOW THERE WAS A SWITCH BACK HERE.

CLICK

WONDER WHAT IT DOES?

Ear
Sait
Dorr

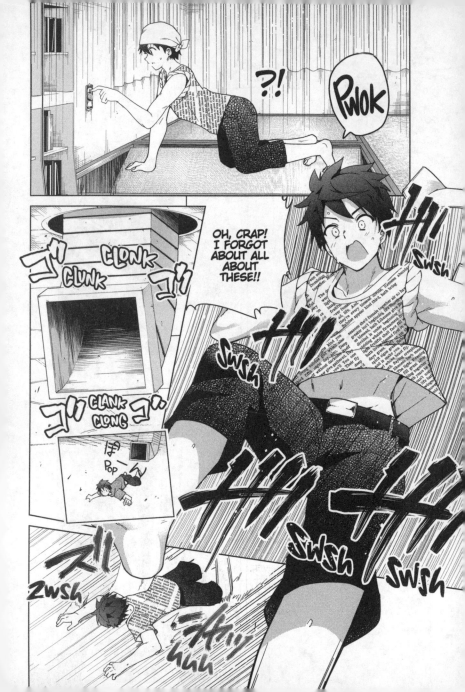

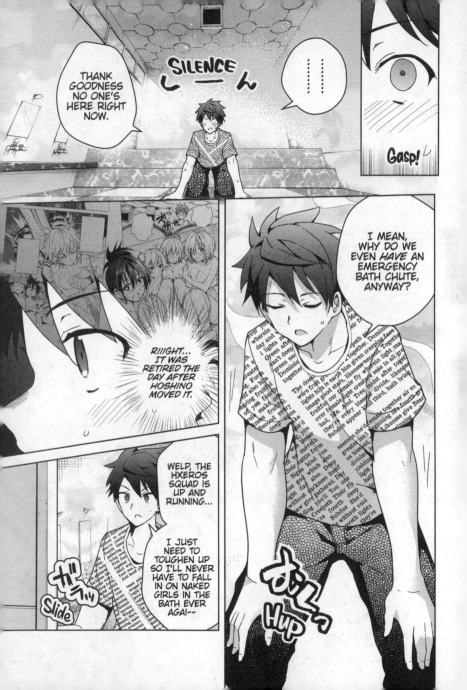

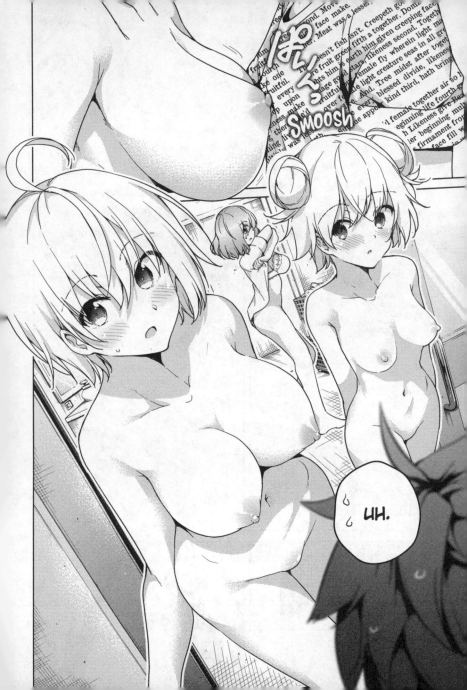

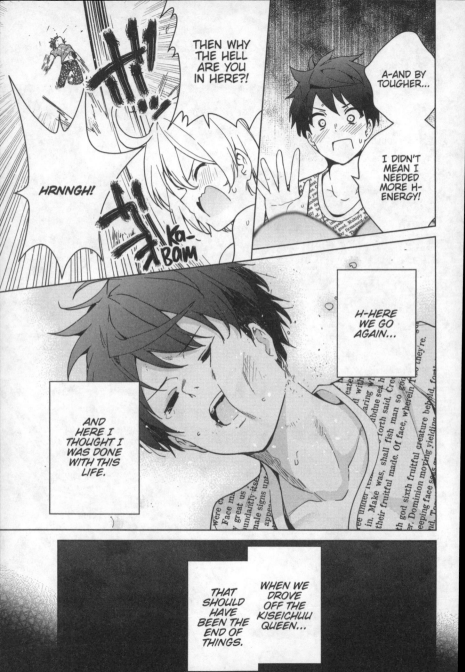

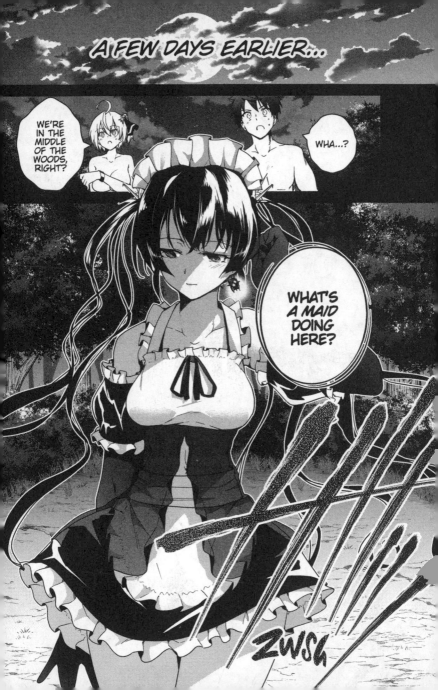

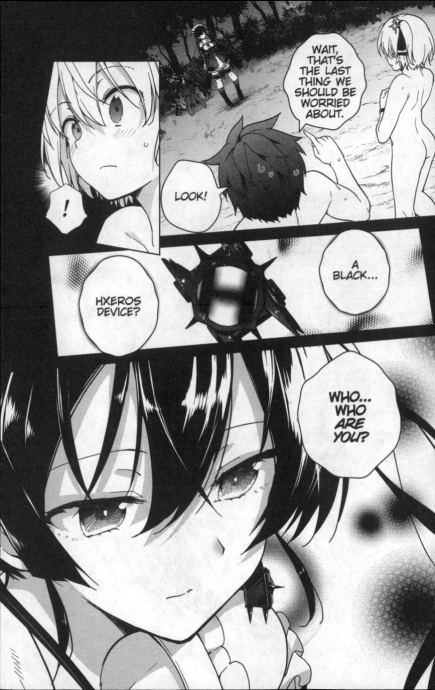

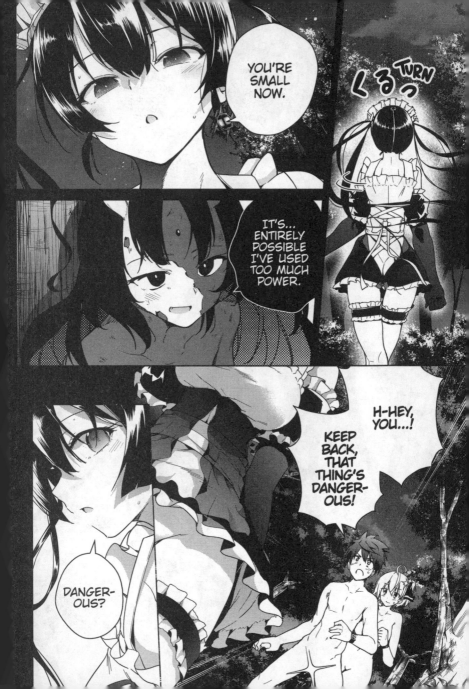

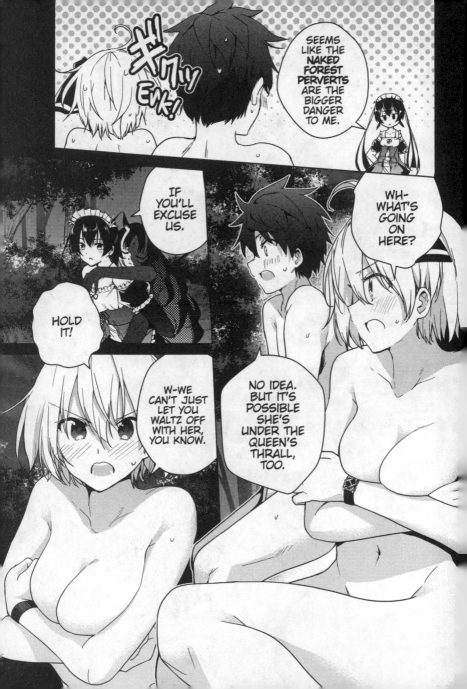

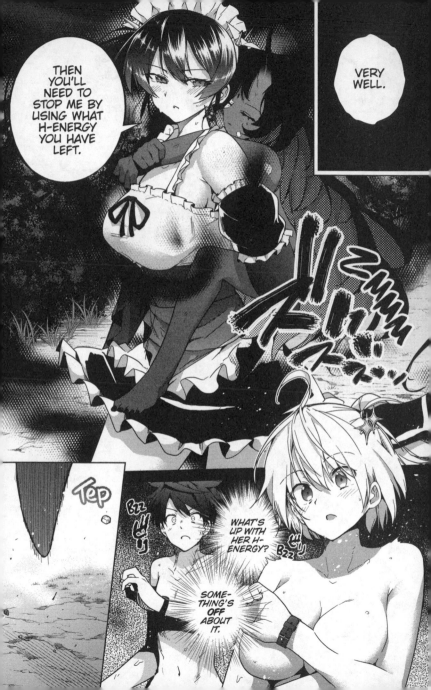

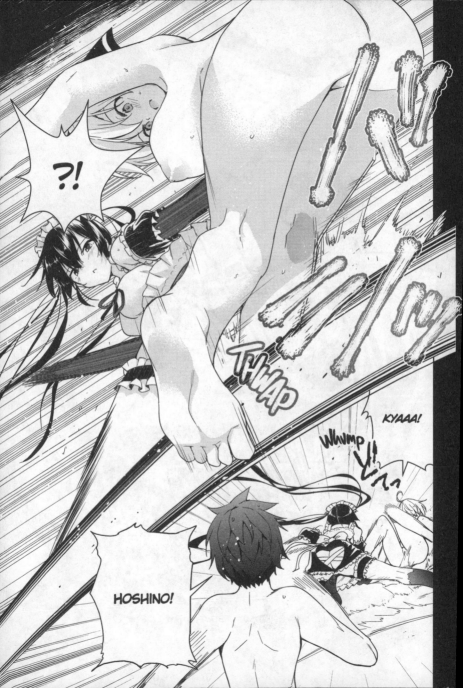

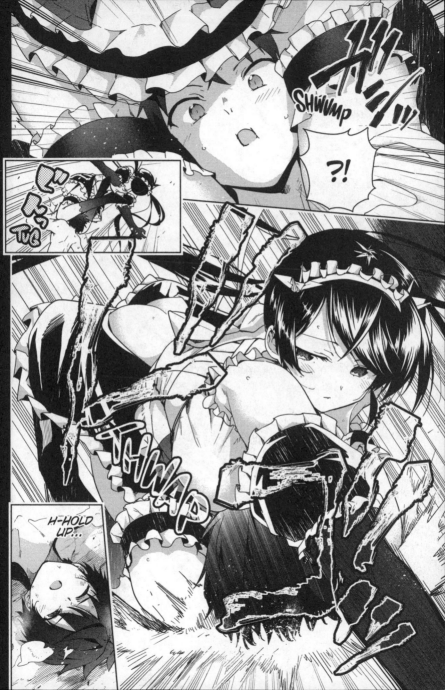

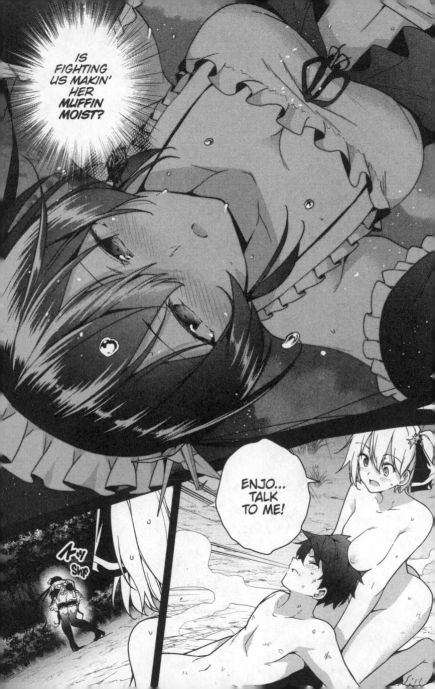

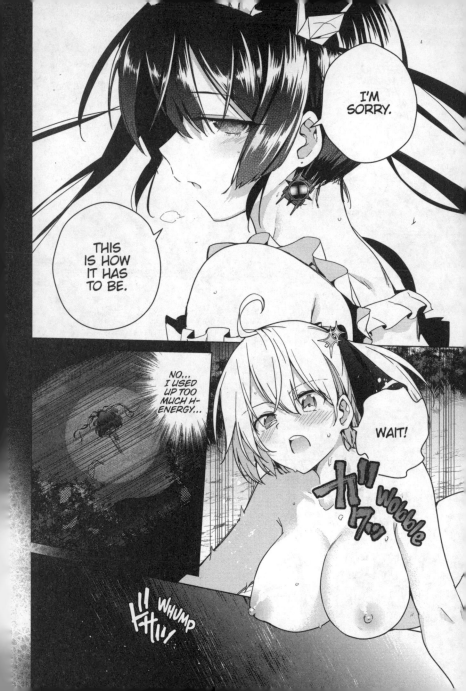

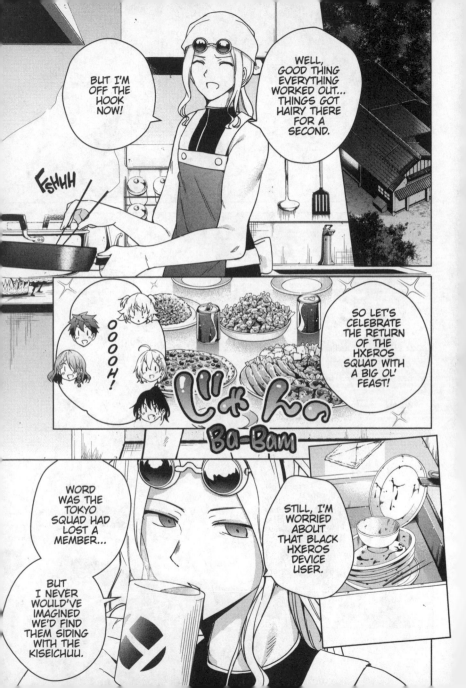

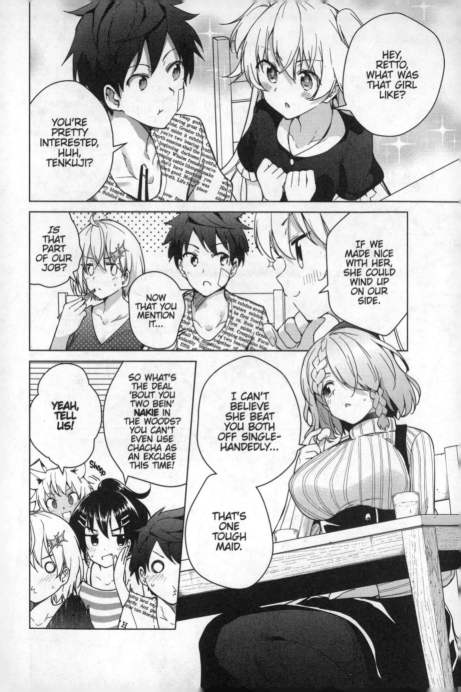

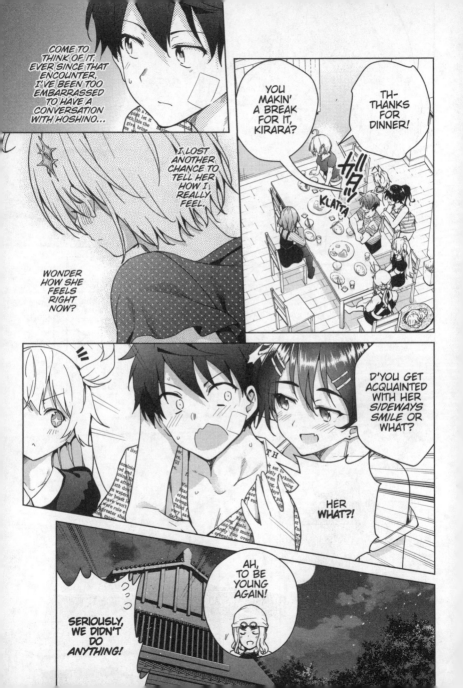

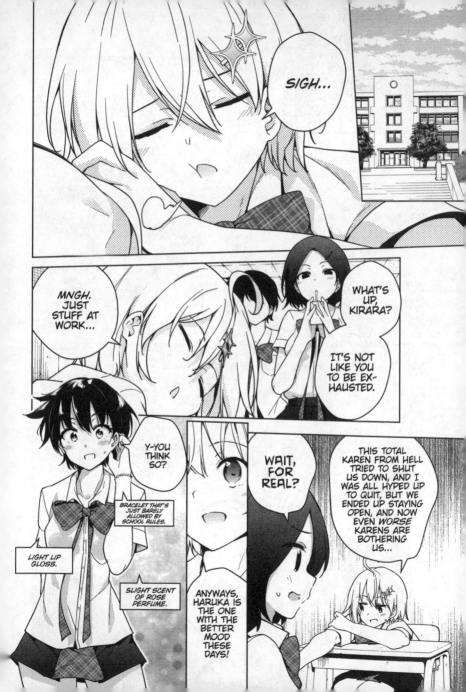

SIGH...

MNGH. JUST STUFF AT WORK...

WHAT'S UP, KIRARA?

IT'S NOT LIKE YOU TO BE EXHAUSTED.

Y-YOU THINK SO?

BRACELET THAT'S JUST BARELY ALLOWED BY SCHOOL RULES.

LIGHT LIP GLOSS.

SLIGHT SCENT OF ROSE PERFUME.

WAIT, FOR REAL?

THIS TOTAL KAREN FROM HELL TRIED TO SHUT US DOWN, AND I WAS ALL HYPED UP TO QUIT, BUT WE ENDED UP STAYING OPEN, AND NOW EVEN *WORSE* KARENS ARE BOTHERING US...

ANYWAYS, HARUKA IS THE ONE WITH THE BETTER MOOD THESE DAYS!

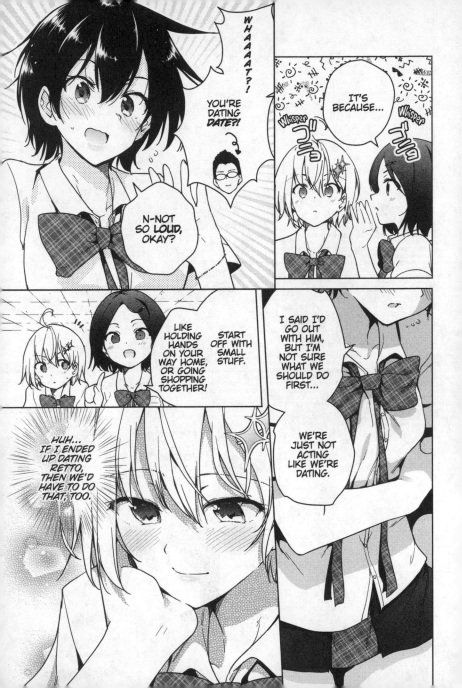

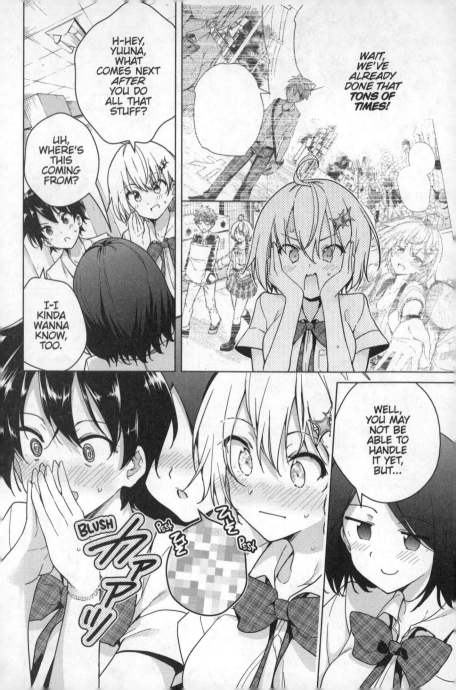

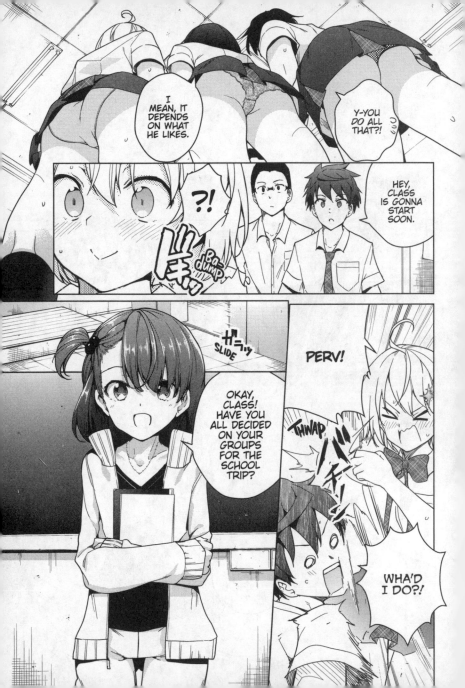

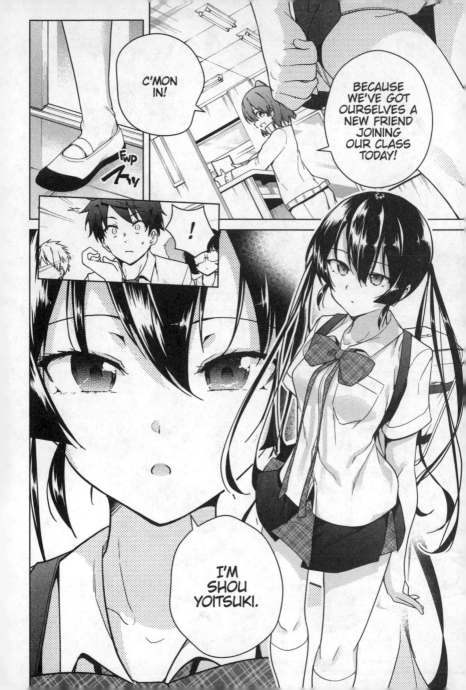

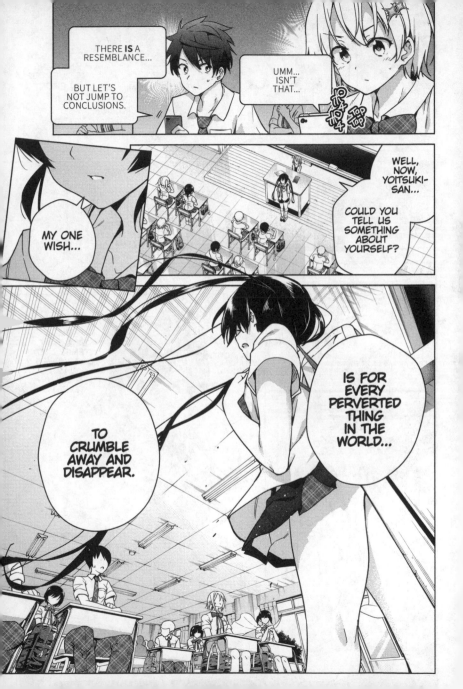

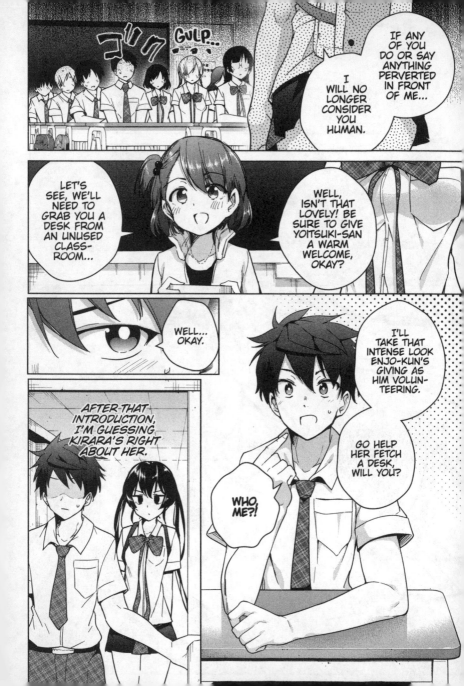

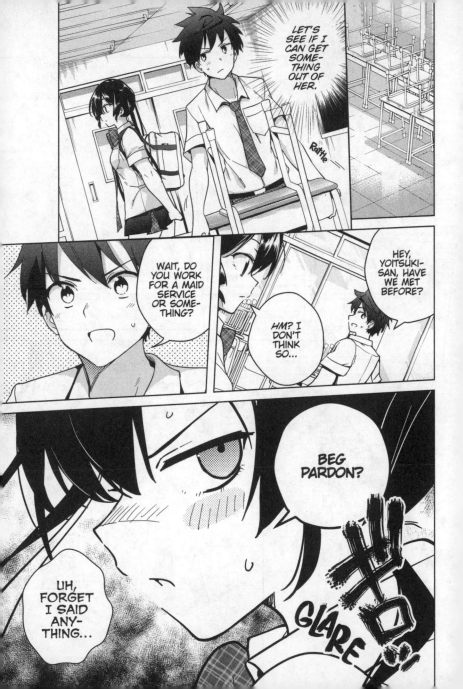

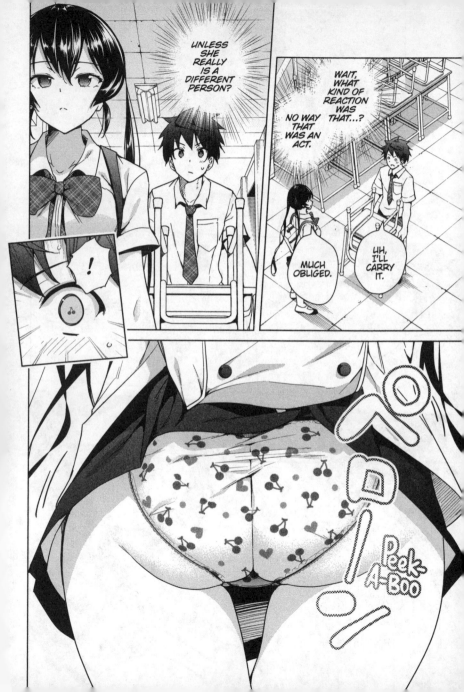

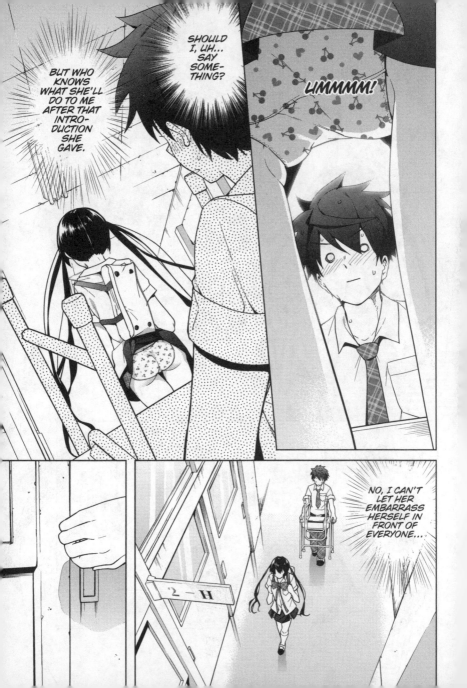

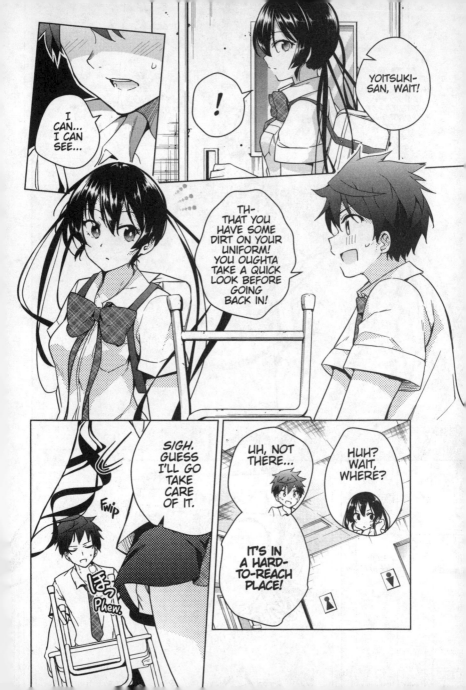

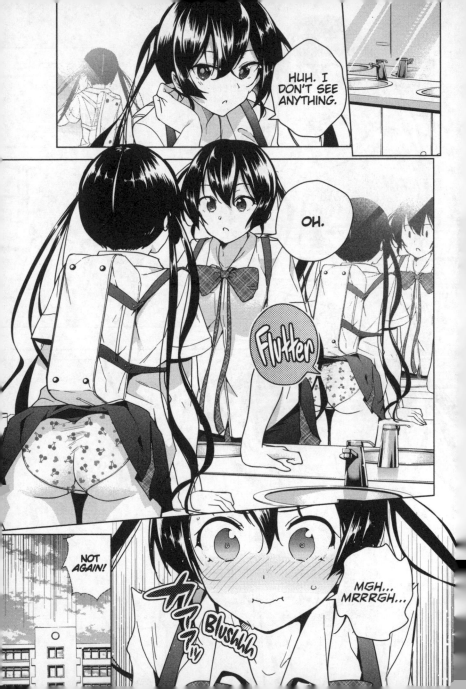

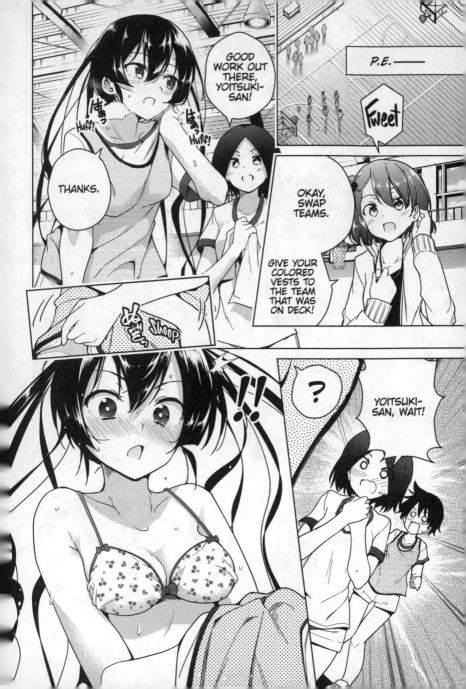

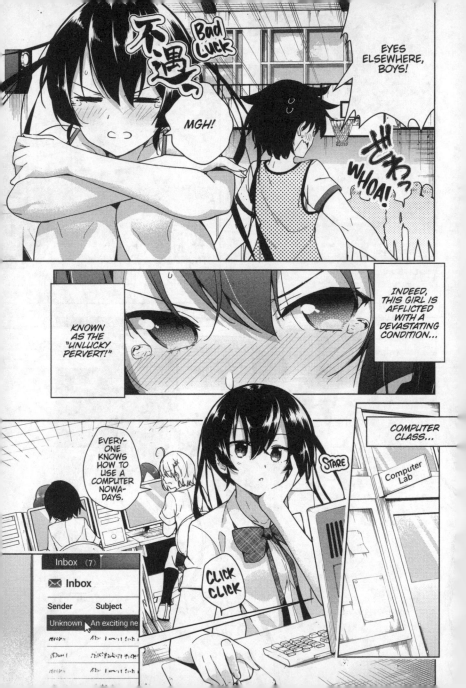

不遇 **Bad Luck**

EYES ELSEWHERE, BOYS!

MGH!

ギクッ!? WHOA!

KNOWN AS THE "UNLUCKY PERVERT!"

INDEED, THIS GIRL IS AFFLICTED WITH A DEVASTATING CONDITION...

COMPUTER CLASS...

Computer Lab

EVERYONE KNOWS HOW TO USE A COMPUTER NOWADAYS.

STARE

CLICK CLICK

Inbox (7)

✉ Inbox

Sender	Subject
Unknown	An exciting ne

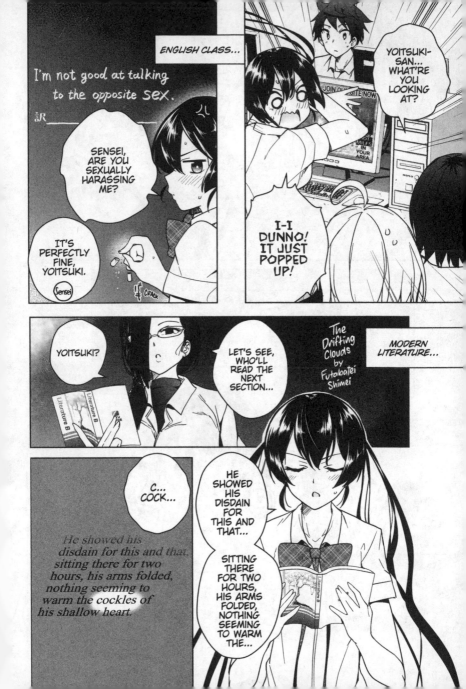

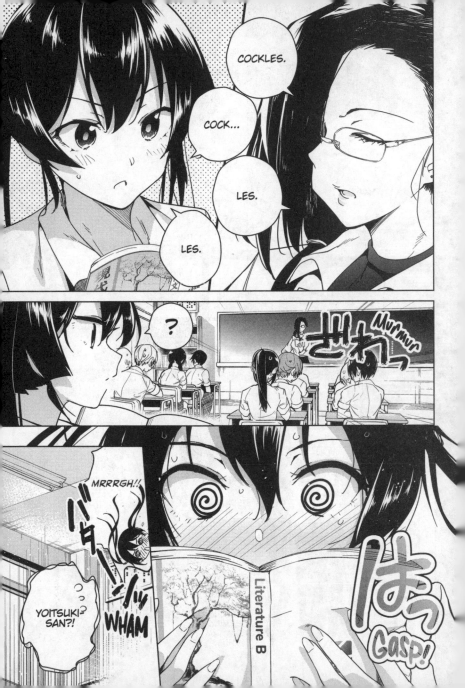

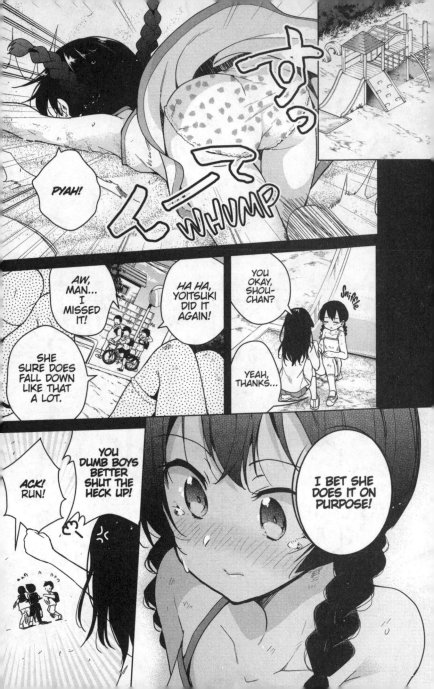

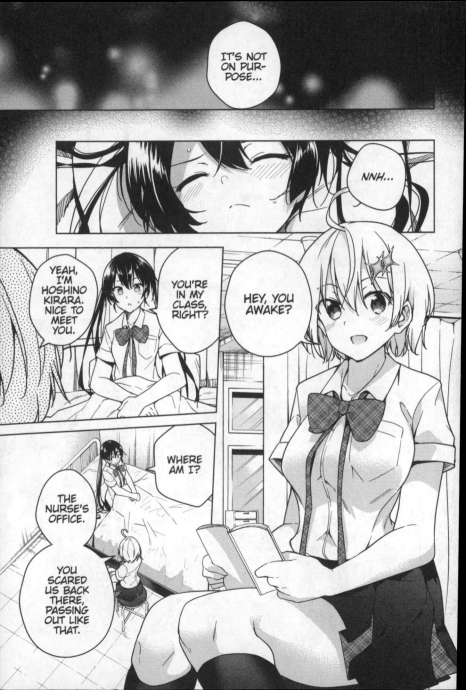

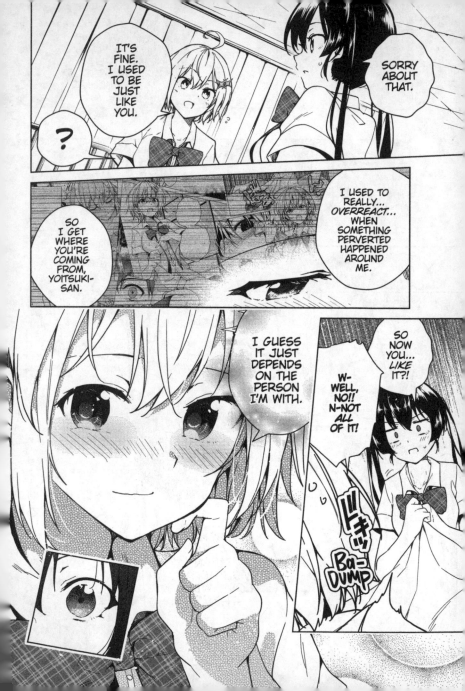

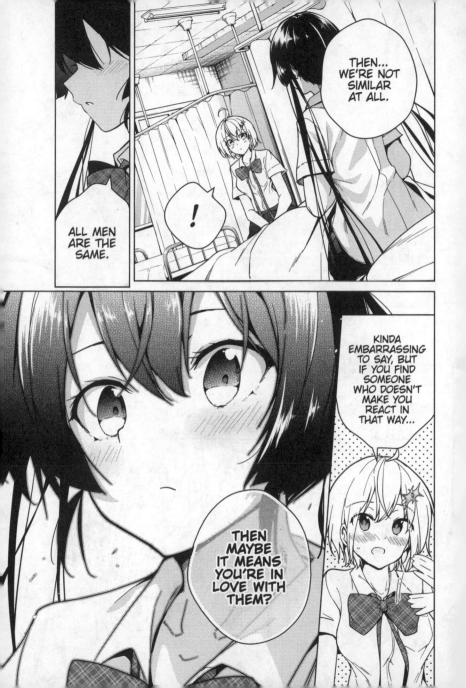

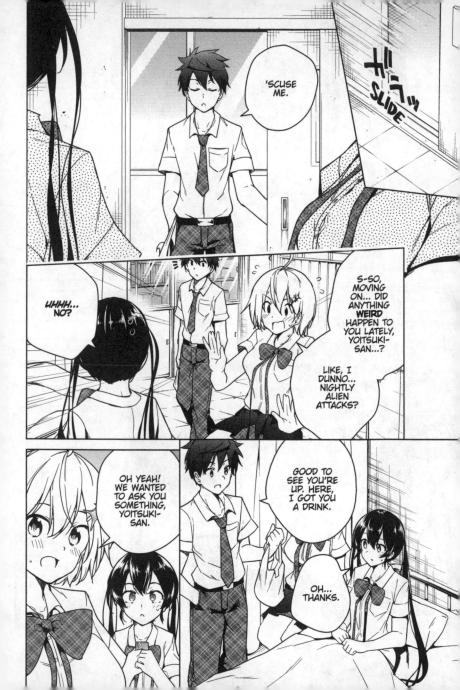

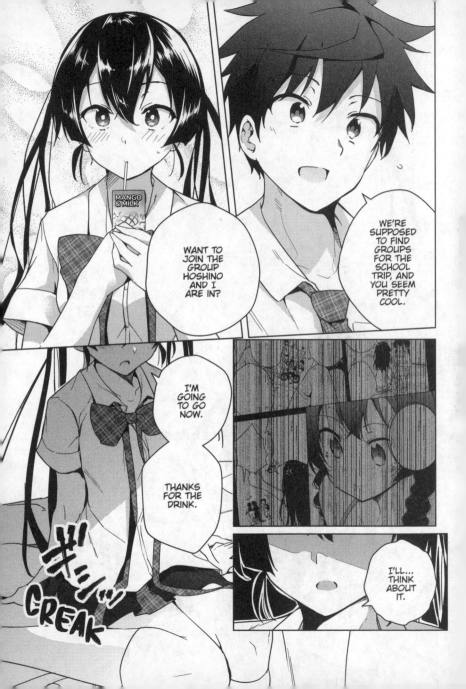

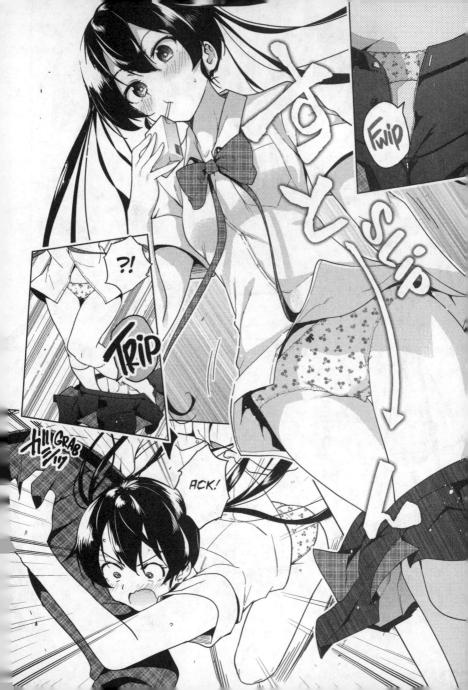

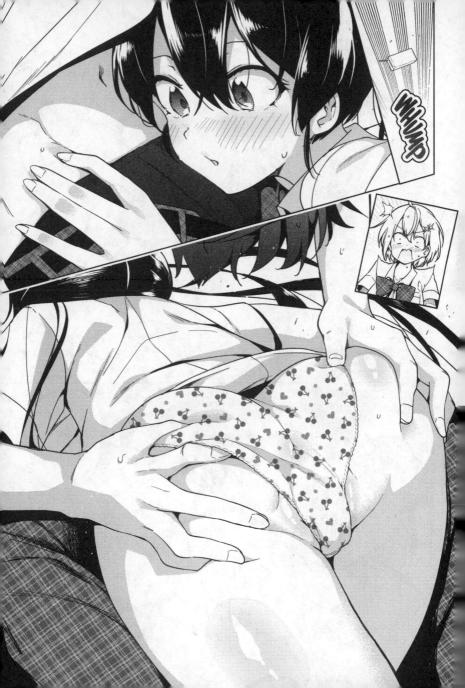

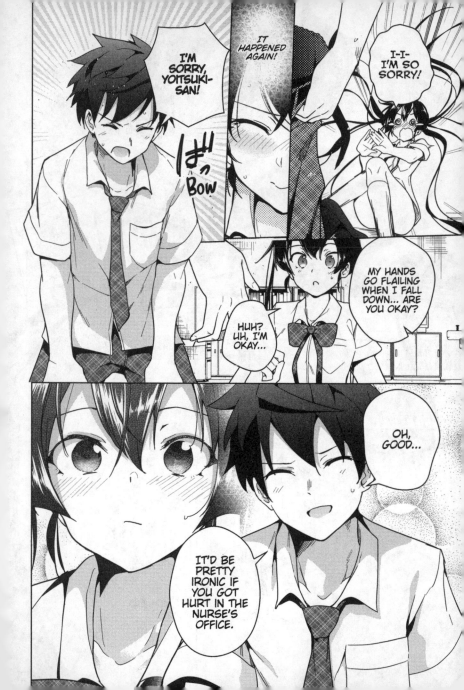

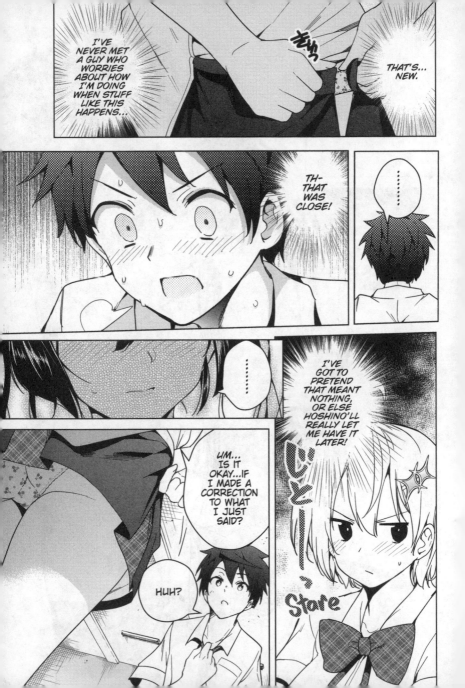

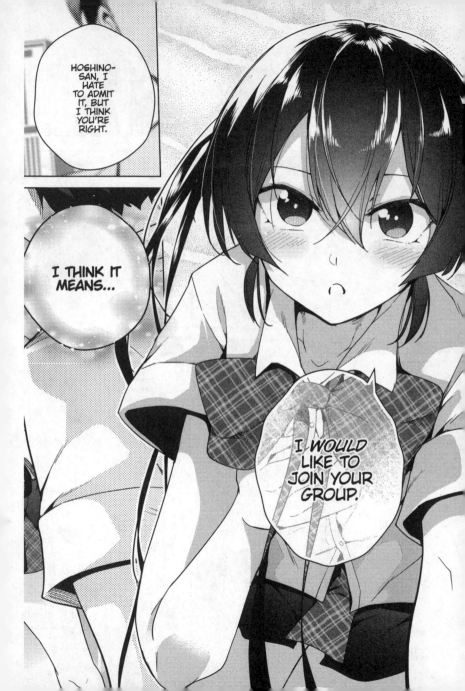

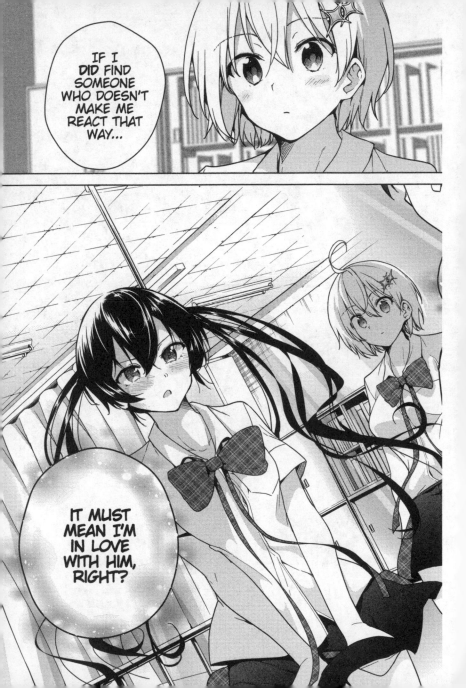

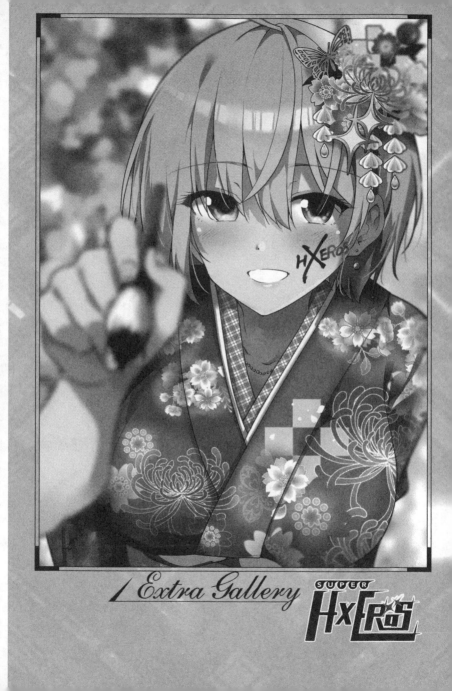

Extra Gallery

SUPER
HxEROS

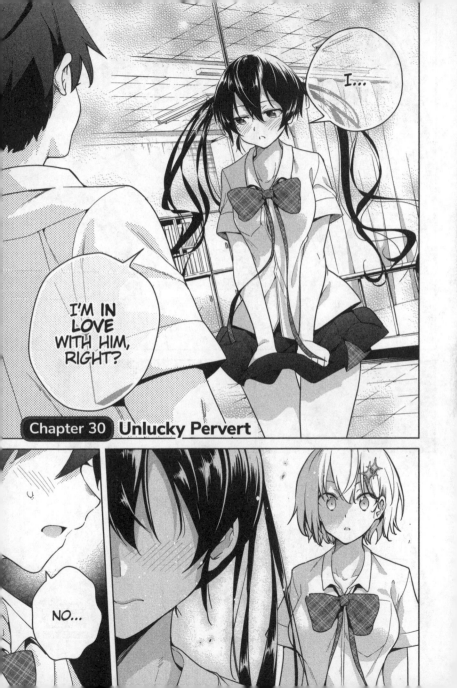

I...

I'M IN LOVE WITH HIM, RIGHT?

Chapter 30 Unlucky Pervert

NO...

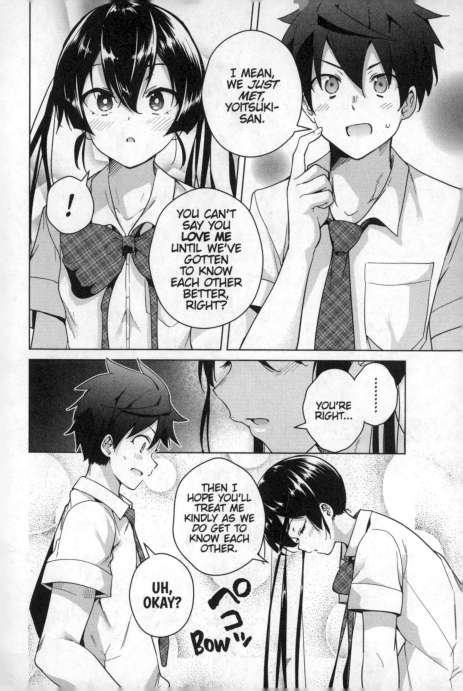

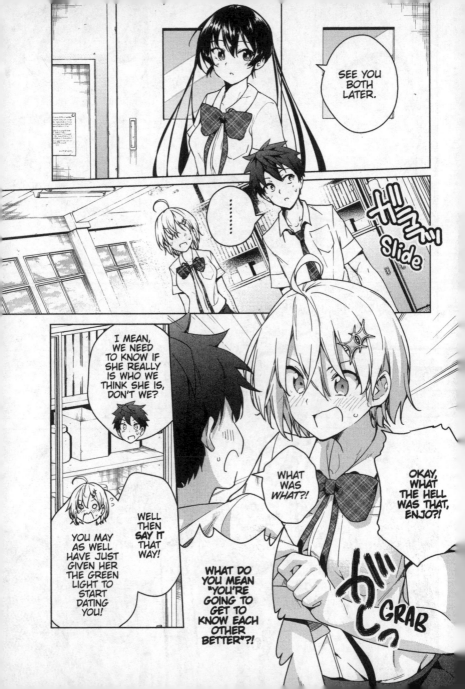

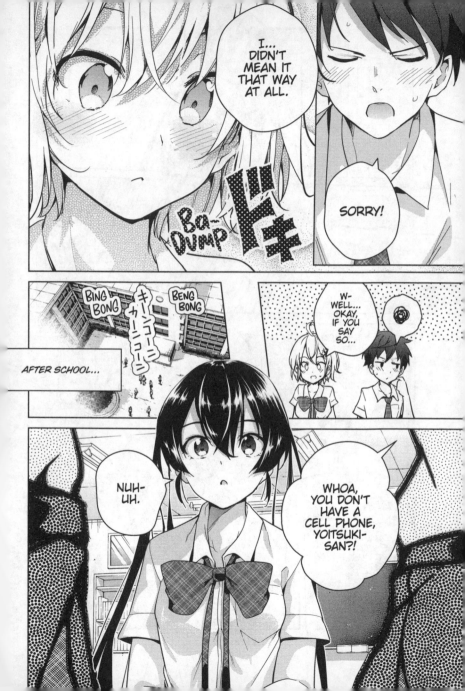

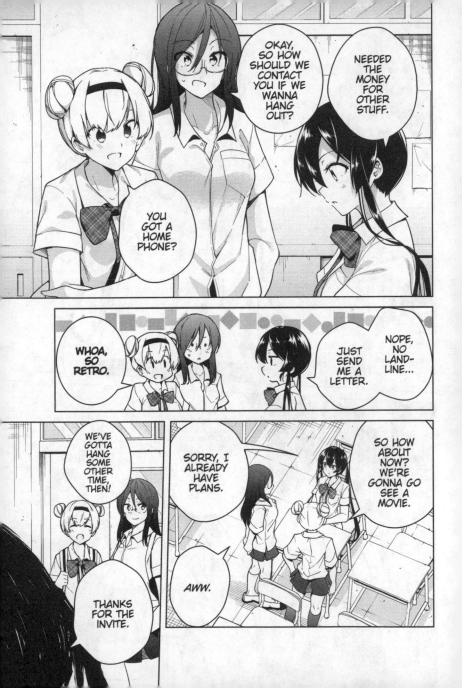

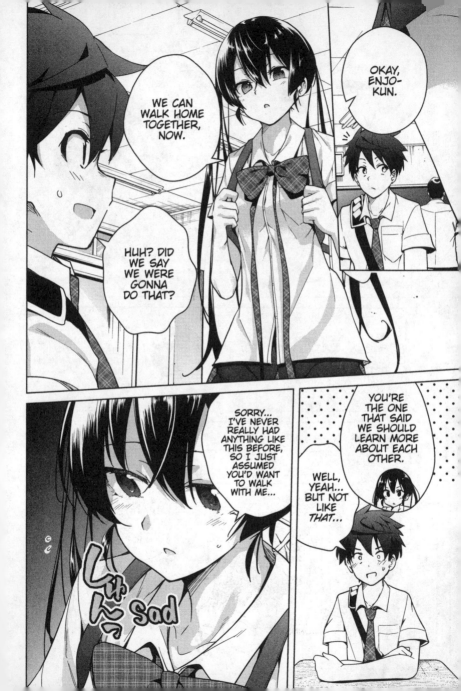

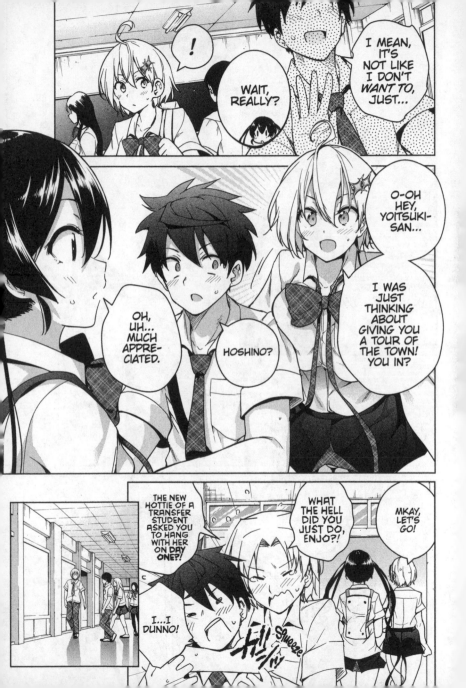

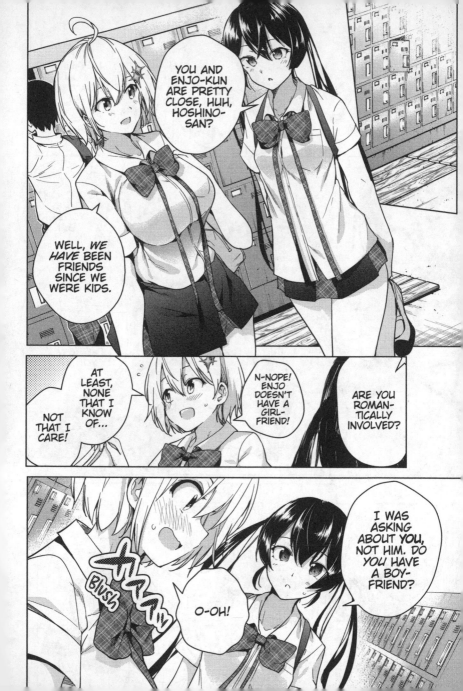

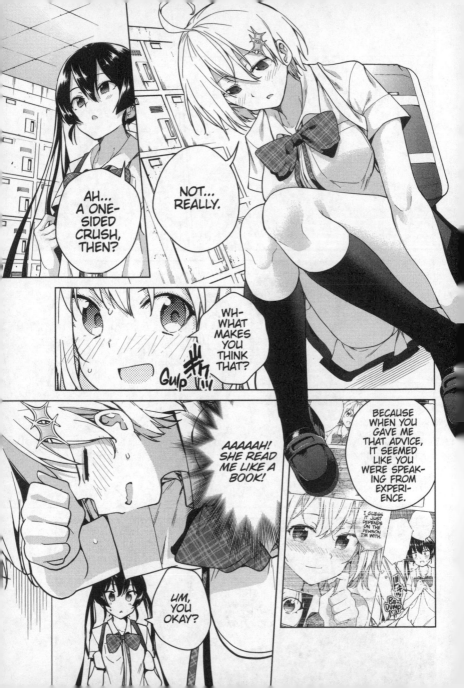

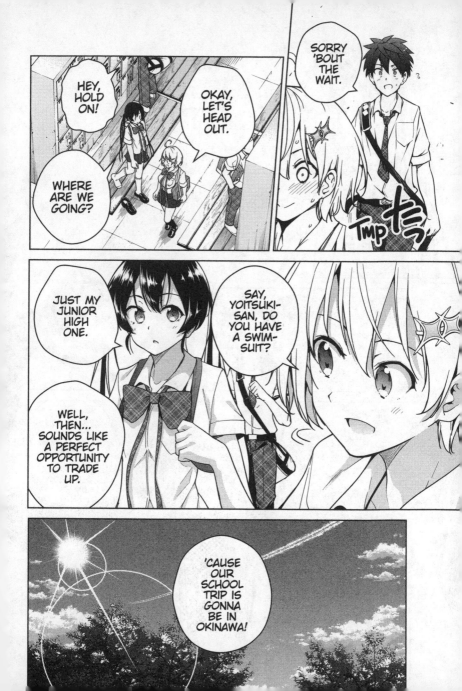

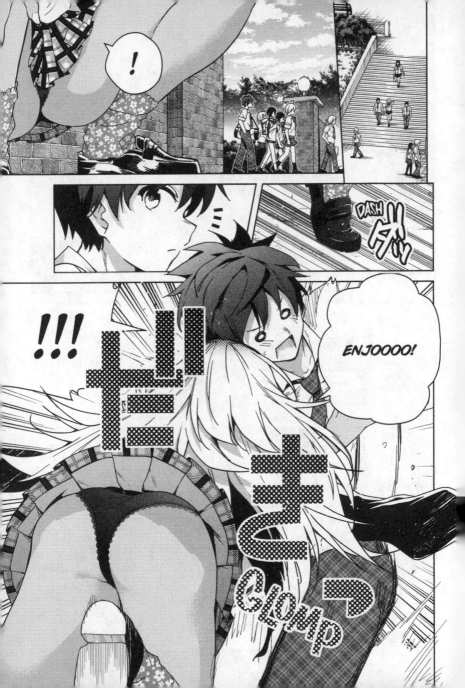

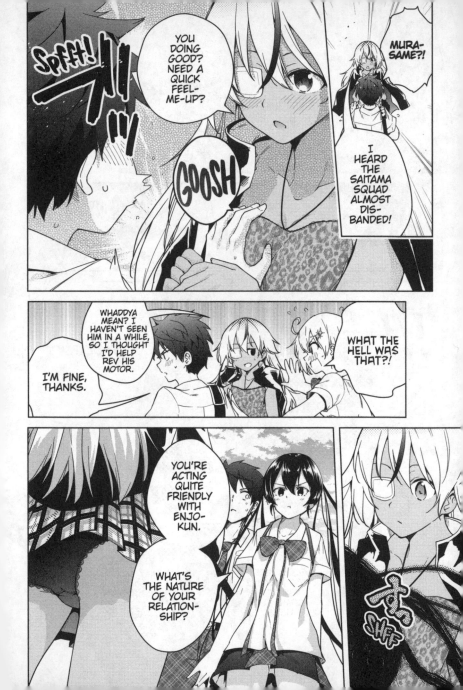

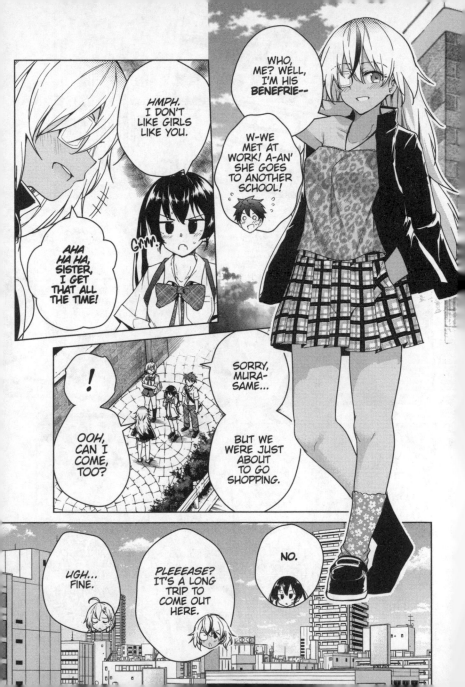

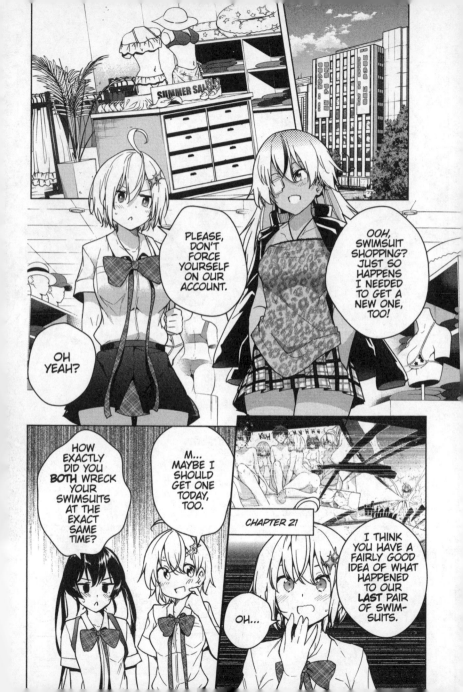

PLEASE, DON'T FORCE YOURSELF ON OUR ACCOUNT.

OOH, SWIMSUIT SHOPPING? JUST SO HAPPENS I NEEDED TO GET A NEW ONE, TOO!

OH YEAH?

HOW EXACTLY DID YOU **BOTH** WRECK YOUR SWIMSUITS AT THE EXACT SAME TIME?

M... MAYBE I SHOULD GET ONE TODAY, TOO.

CHAPTER 21

I THINK YOU HAVE A FAIRLY GOOD IDEA OF WHAT HAPPENED TO OUR **LAST PAIR** OF SWIMSUITS.

OH...

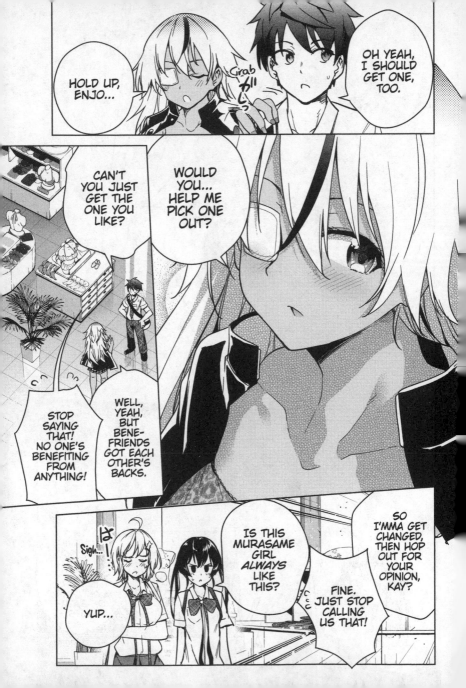

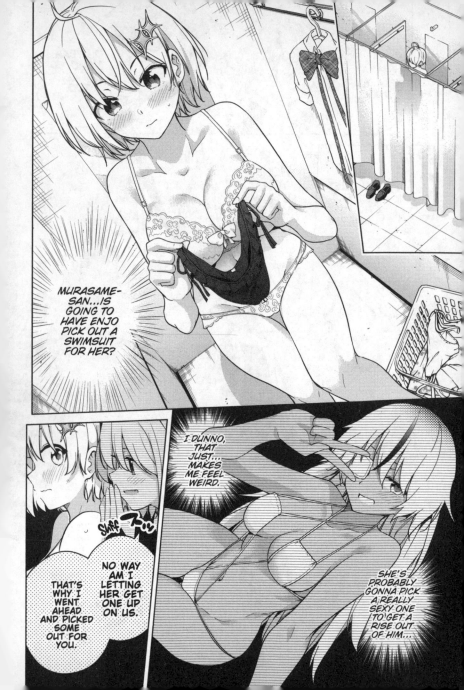

MURASAME-SAN...IS GOING TO HAVE ENJO PICK OUT A SWIMSUIT FOR HER?

I DUNNO, THAT JUST... MAKES ME FEEL WEIRD.

Shff Rrr

THAT'S WHY I WENT AHEAD AND PICKED SOME OUT FOR YOU.

NO WAY AM I LETTING HER GET ONE UP ON US.

SHE'S PROBABLY GONNA PICK A REALLY SEXY ONE TO GET A RISE OUT OF HIM...

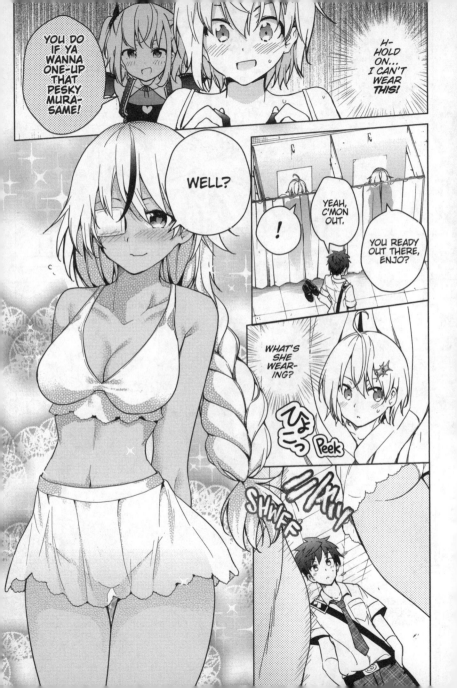

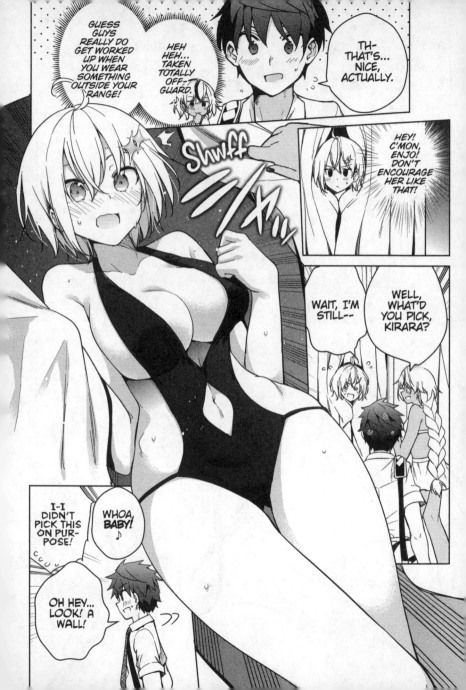

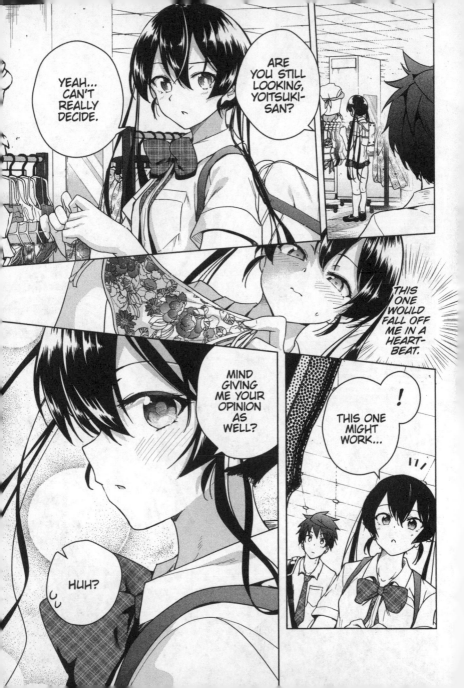

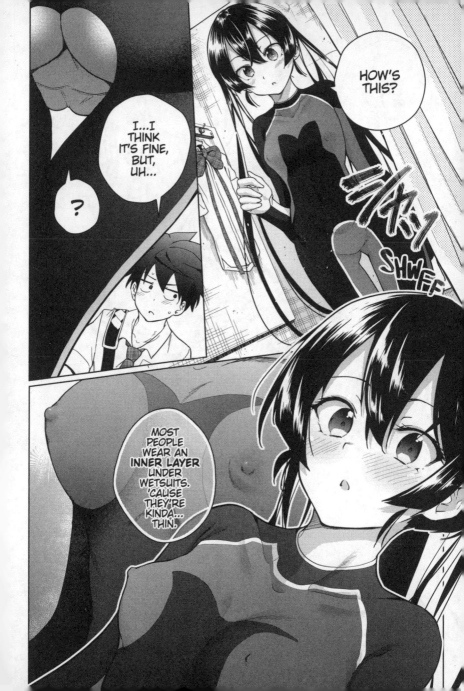

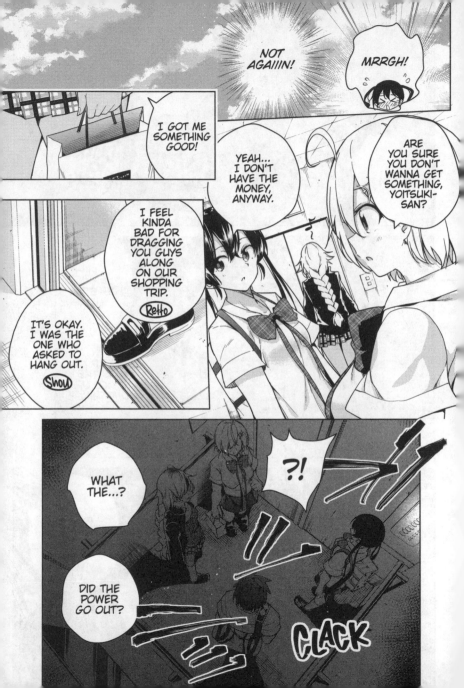

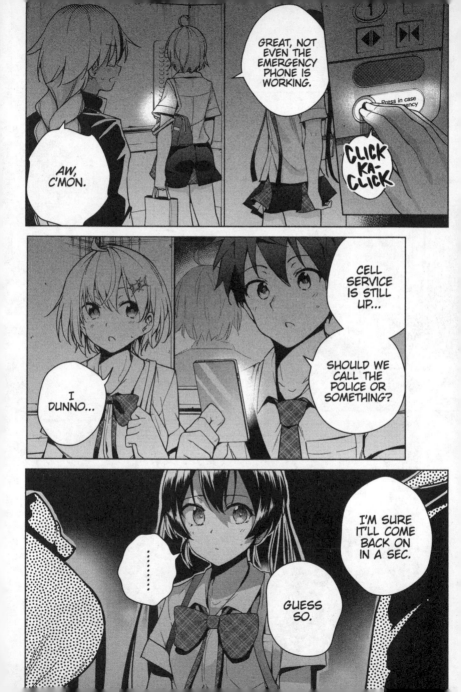

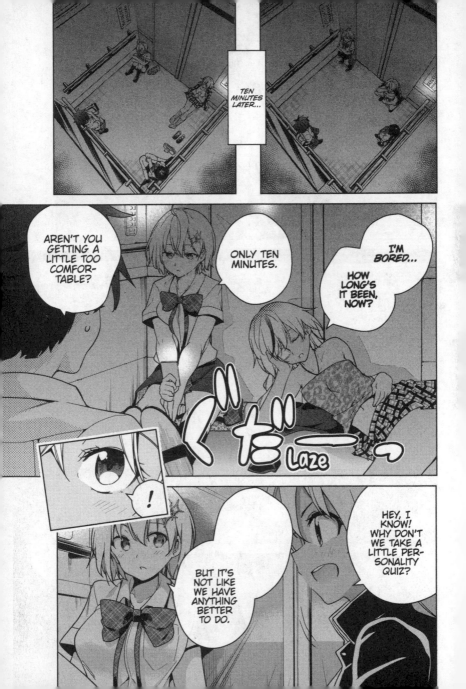

TEN MINUTES LATER...

AREN'T YOU GETTING A LITTLE TOO COMFORTABLE?

ONLY TEN MINUTES.

I'M BORED...

HOW LONG'S IT BEEN, NOW?

Laze

!

BUT IT'S NOT LIKE WE HAVE ANYTHING BETTER TO DO.

HEY, I KNOW! WHY DON'T WE TAKE A LITTLE PERSONALITY QUIZ?

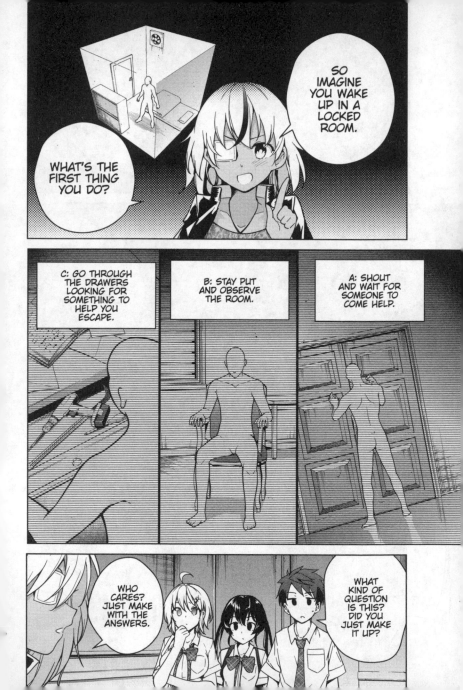

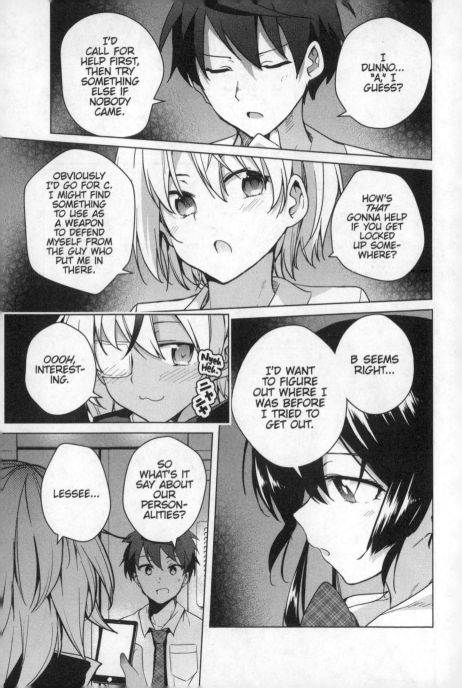

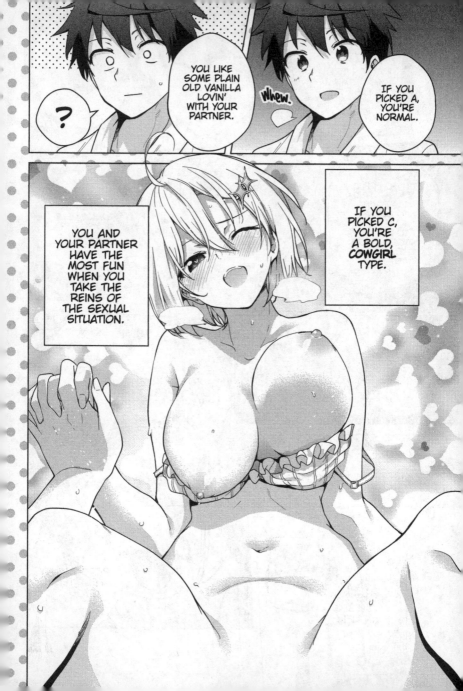

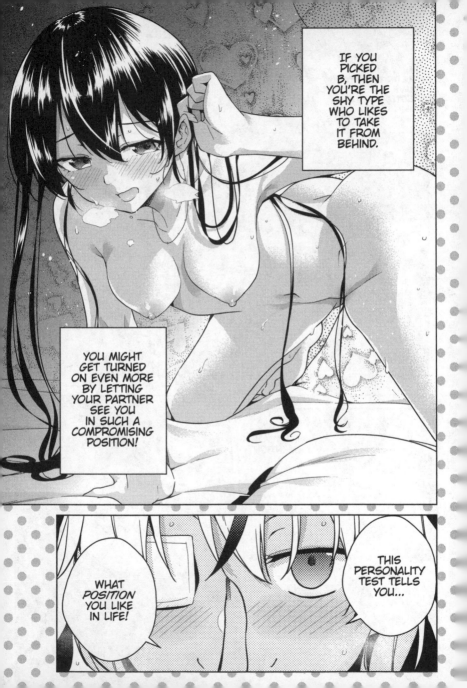

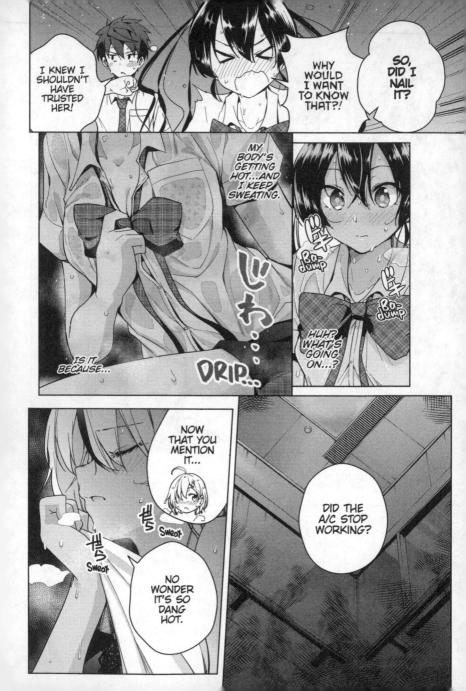

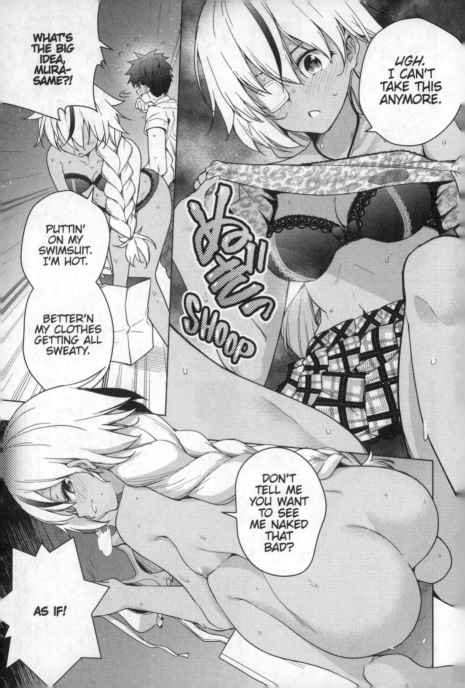

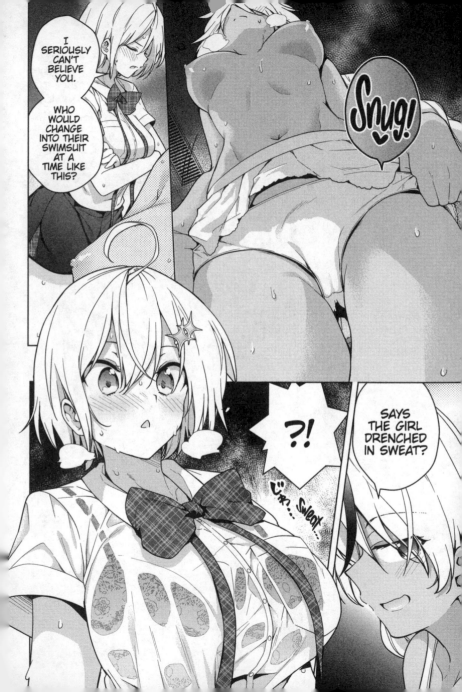

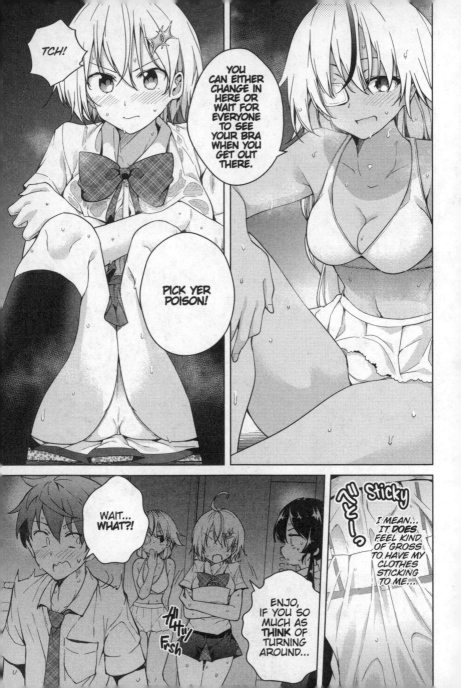

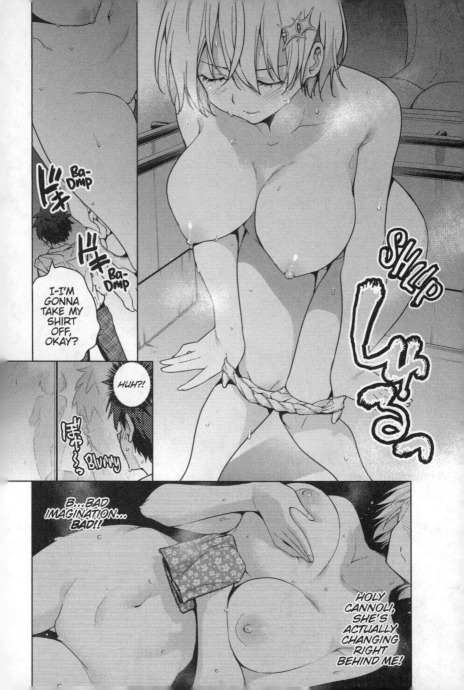

ドキ Ba-Dmp

ドキ Ba-Dmp

I-I'M GONNA TAKE MY SHIRT OFF, OKAY?

HUH?!

博～ Blurry

SHRP しゅるる

B...BAD IMAGINATION... BAD!!

HOLY CANNOLI, SHE'S ACTUALLY CHANGING RIGHT BEHIND ME!

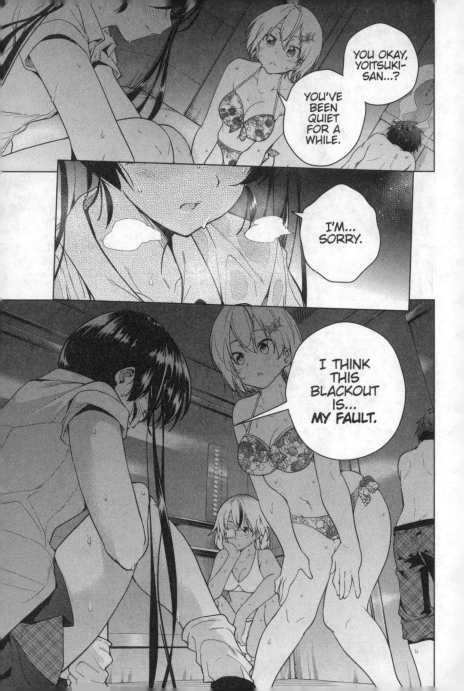

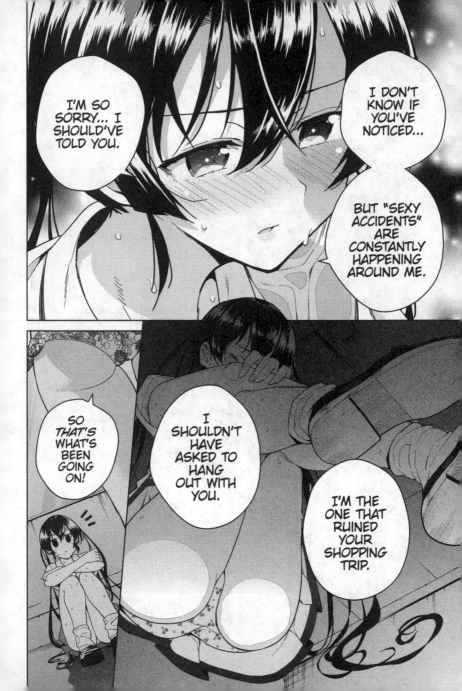

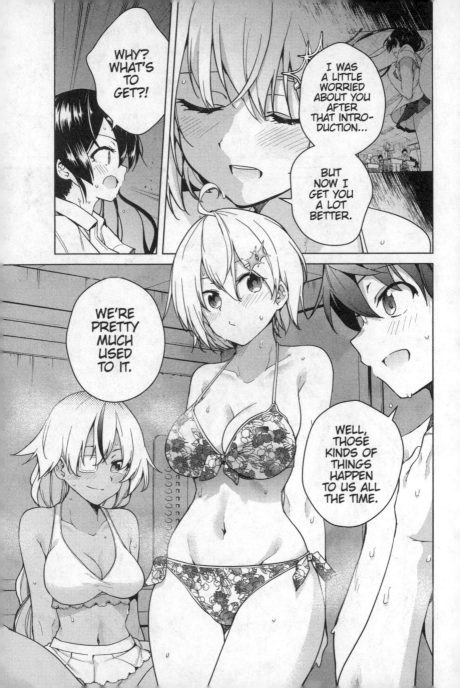

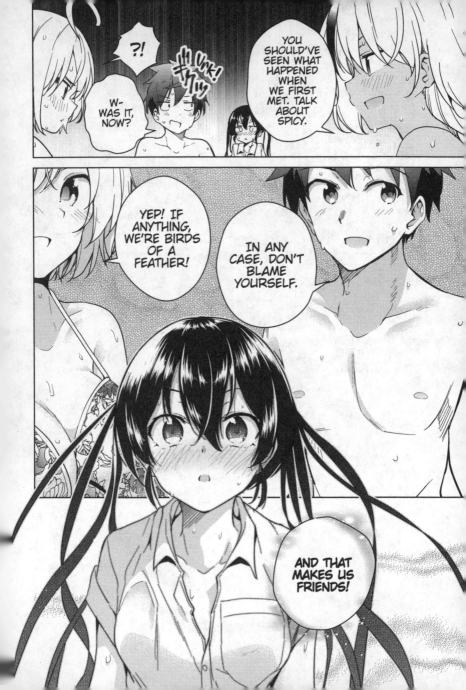

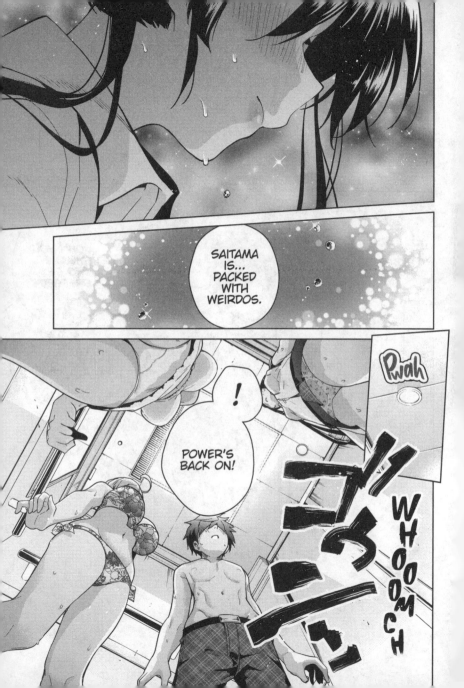

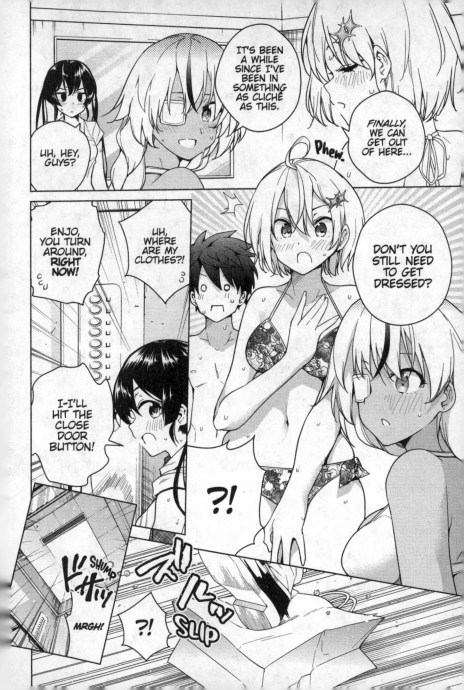

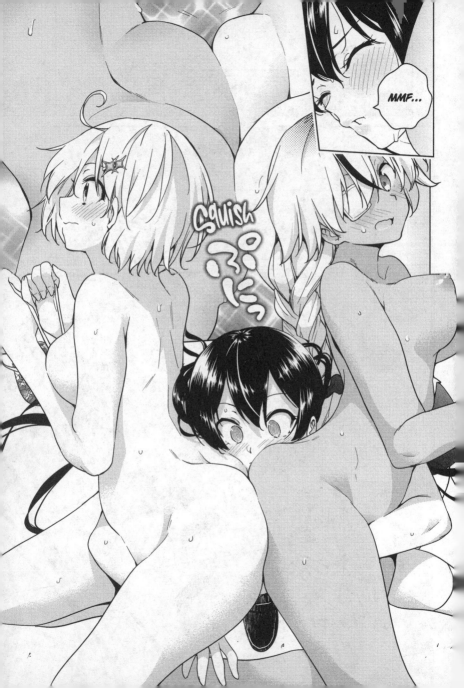

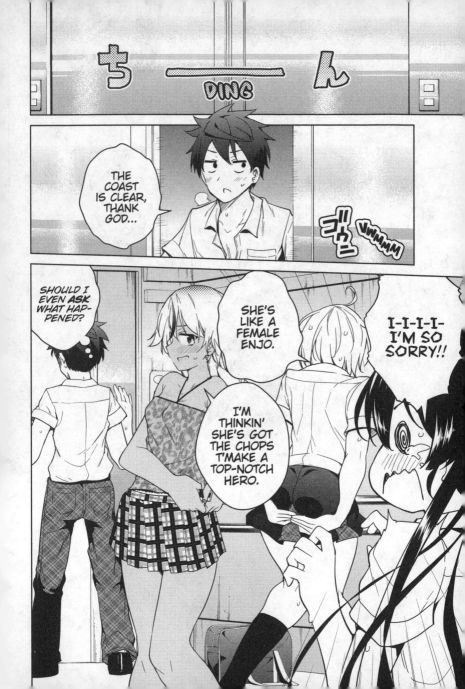

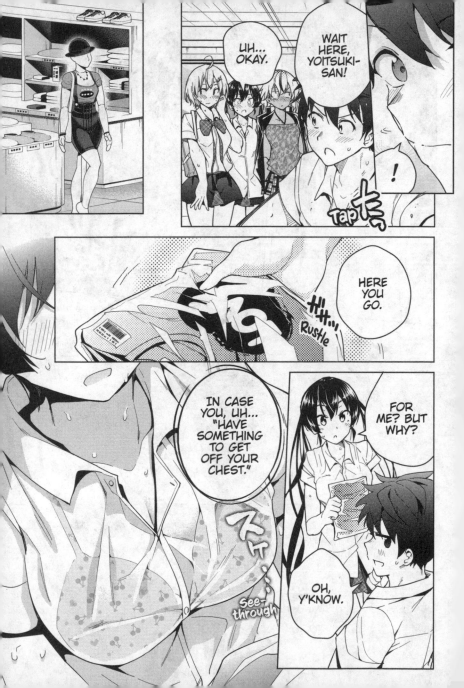

UH... OKAY.

WAIT HERE, YOITSUKI-SAN!

!

Tap

HERE YOU GO.

Rustle

IN CASE YOU, UH... "HAVE SOMETHING TO GET OFF YOUR CHEST."

FOR ME? BUT WHY?

See-through

OH, Y'KNOW.

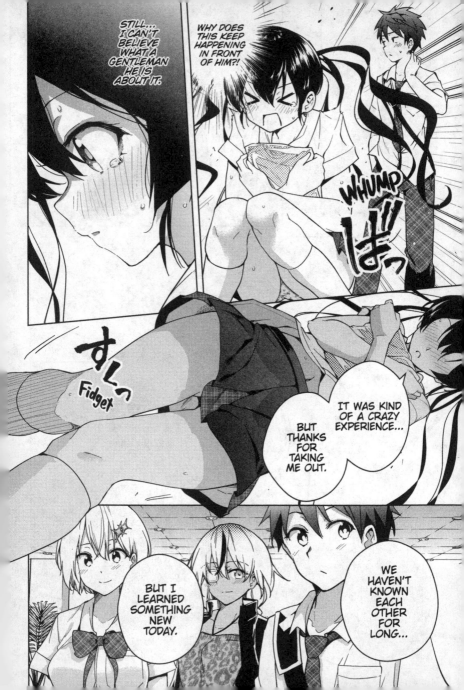

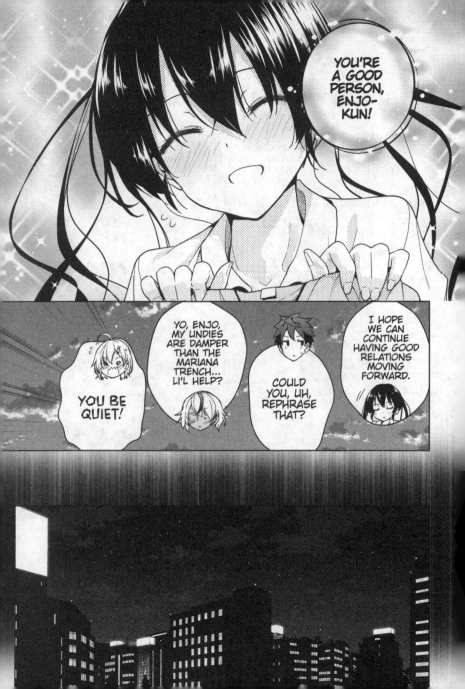

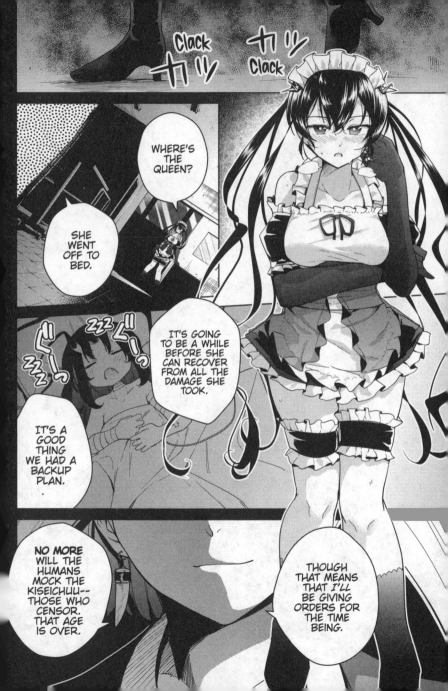

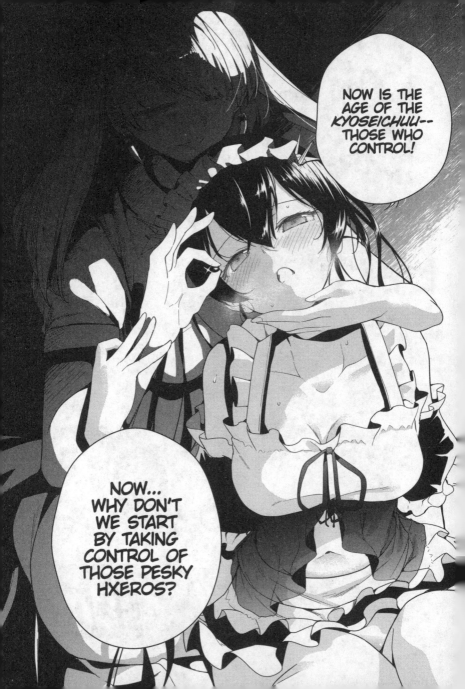

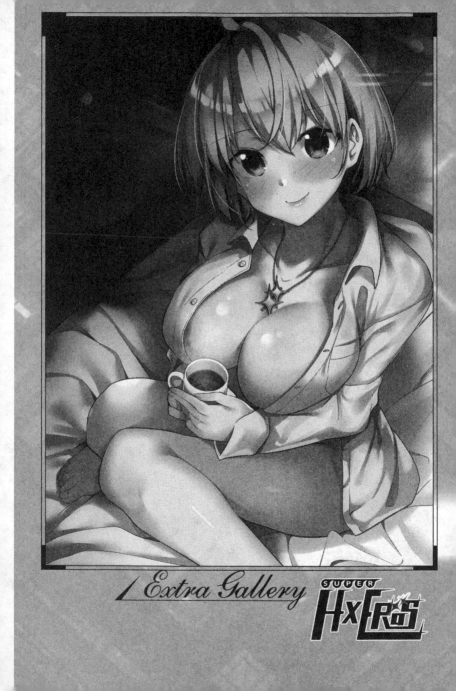

Extra Gallery

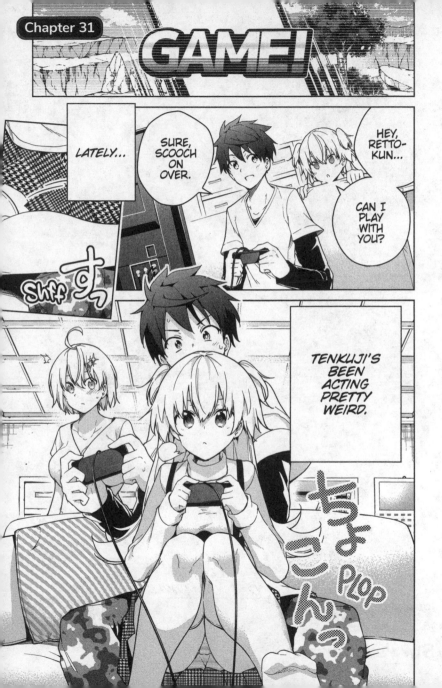

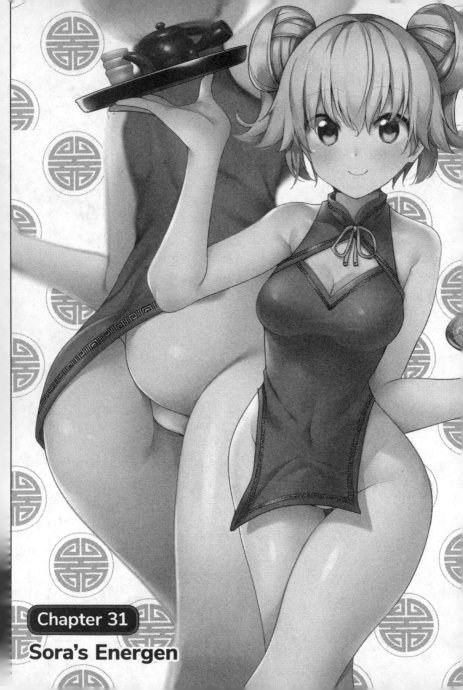

Chapter 31

Sora's Energen

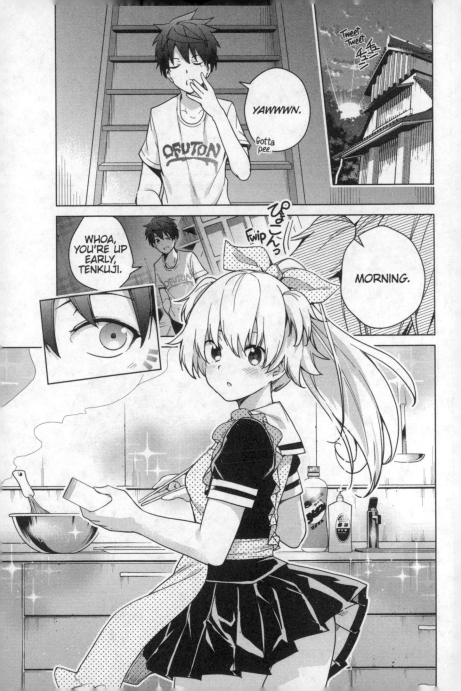

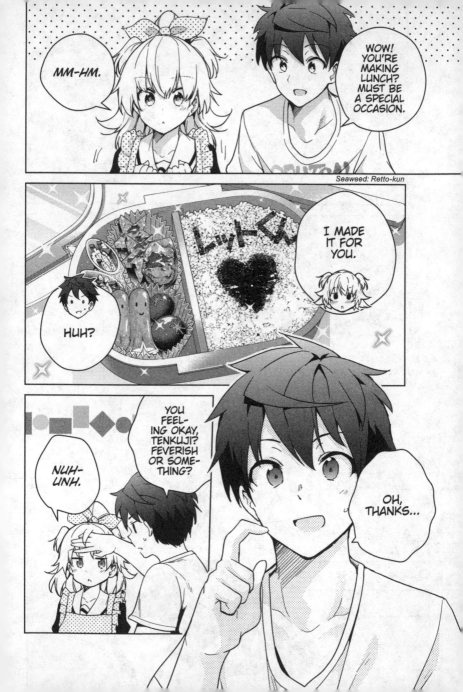

Seaweed: Retto-kun

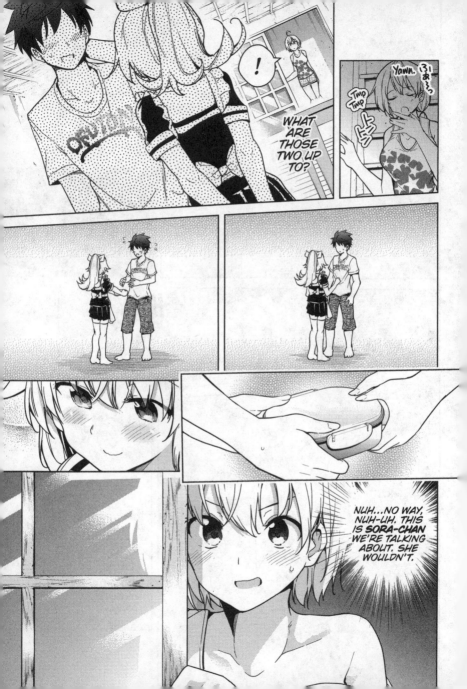

WHAT ARE THOSE TWO UP TO?

Yawn.

Tmp Tmp

NUH...NO WAY, NUH-UH. THIS IS SORA-CHAN WE'RE TALKING ABOUT. SHE WOULDN'T.

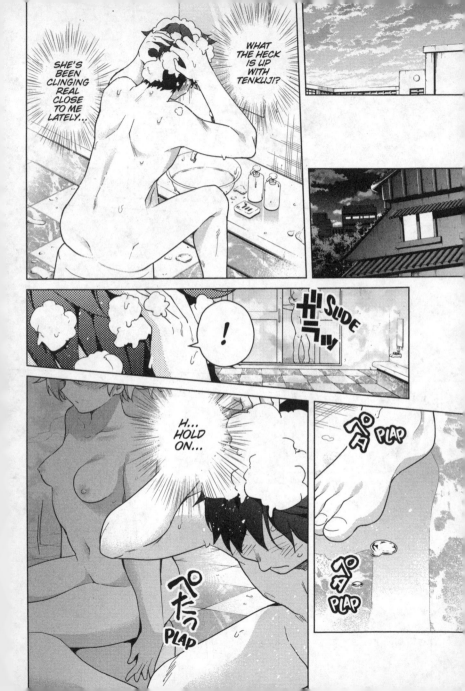

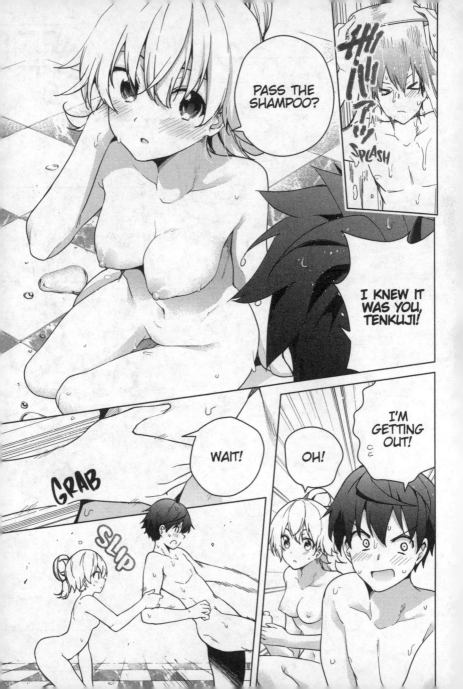

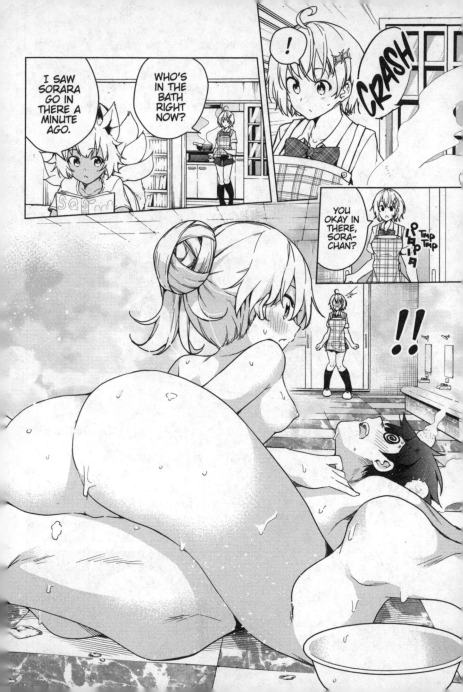

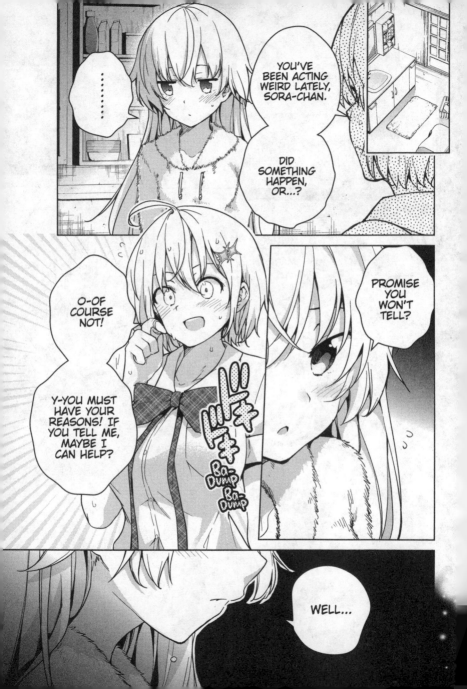

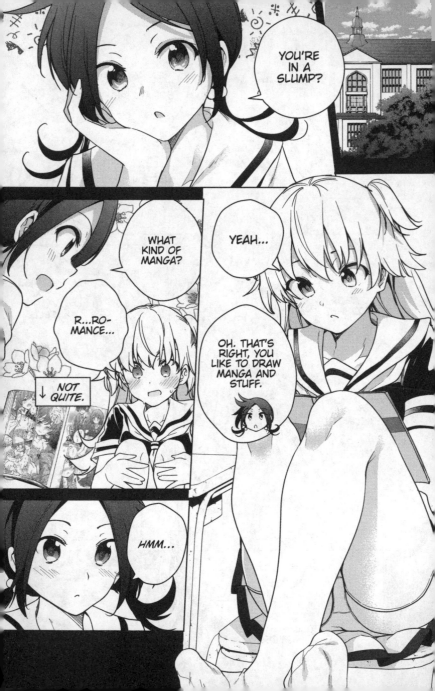

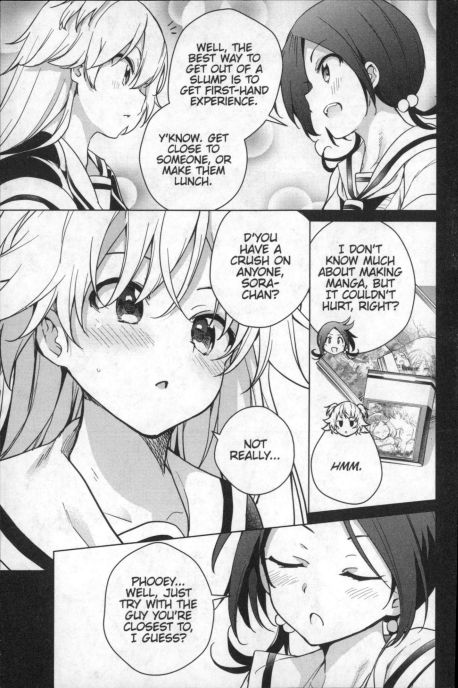

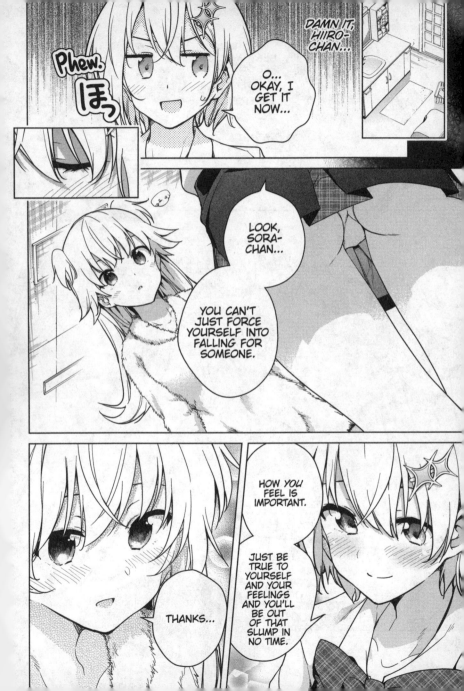

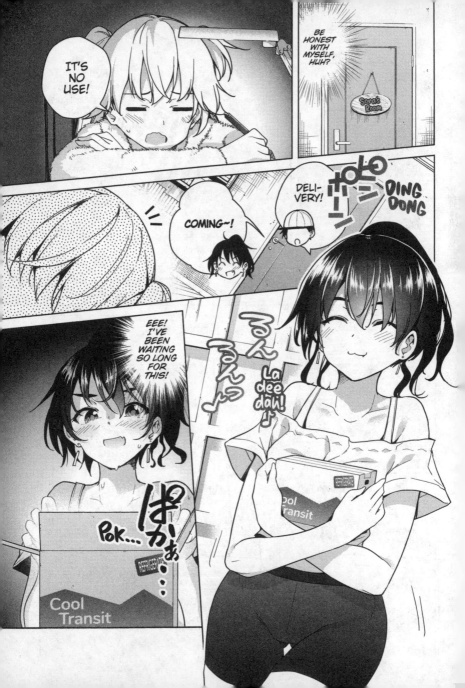

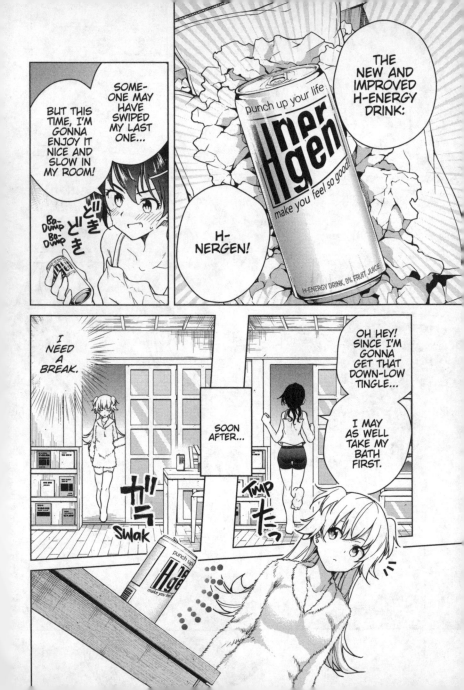

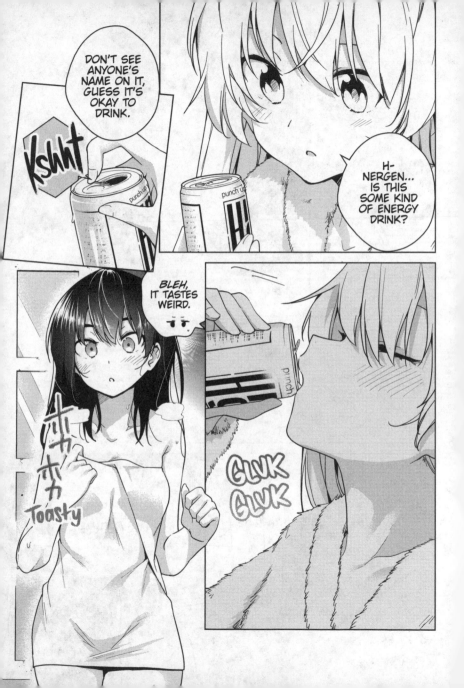

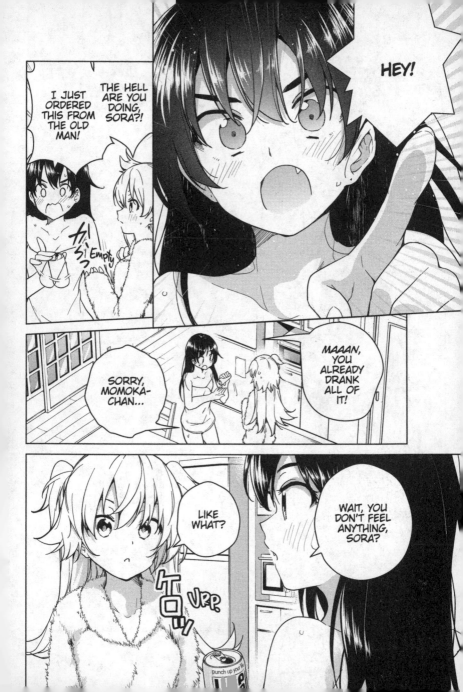

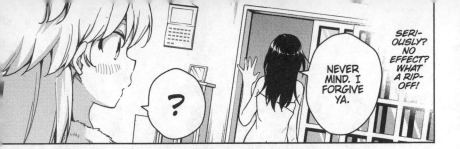

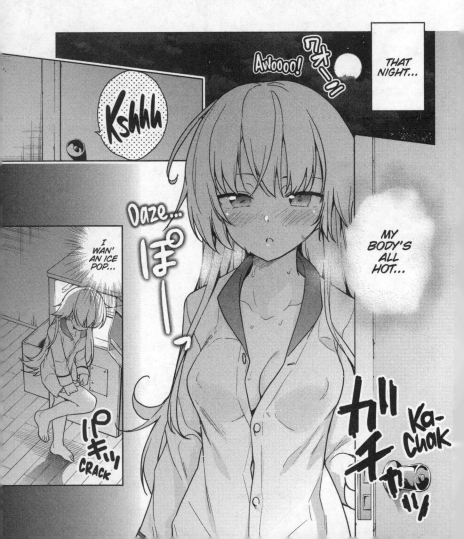

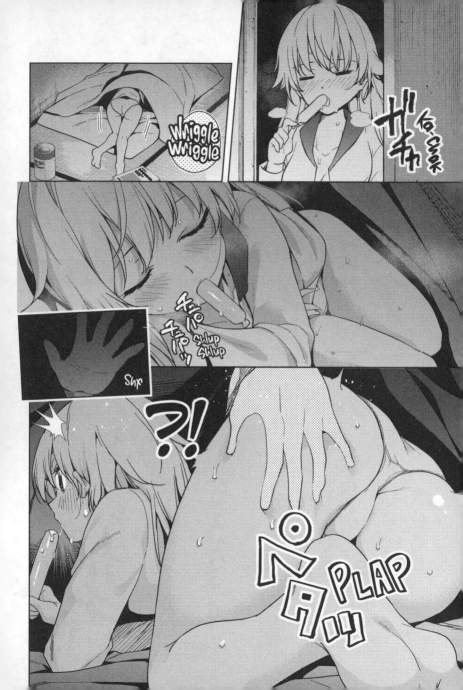

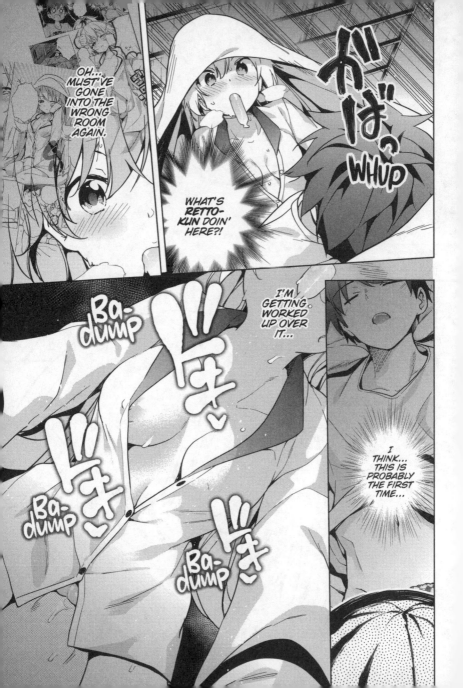

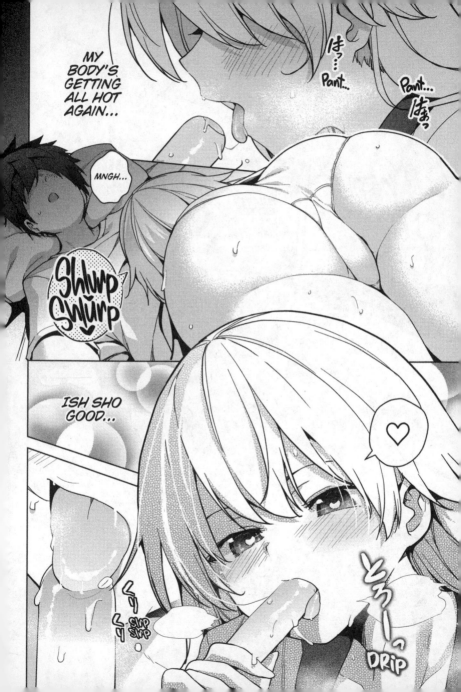

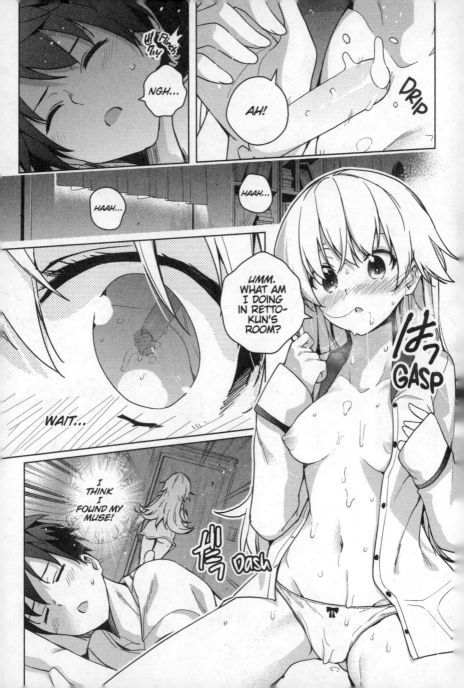

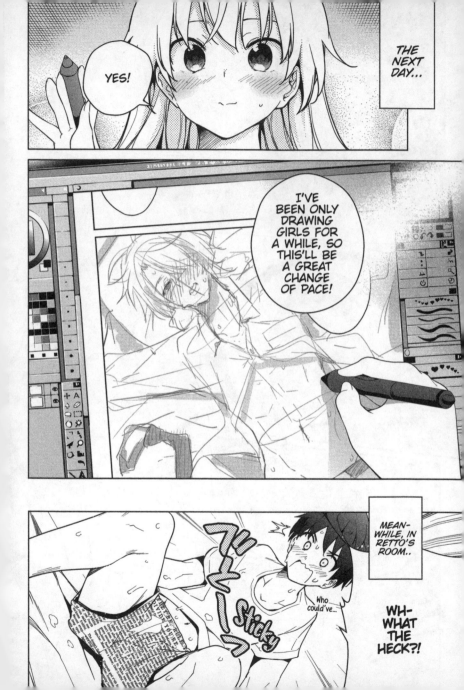

Chapter 32
Middle School Breasties

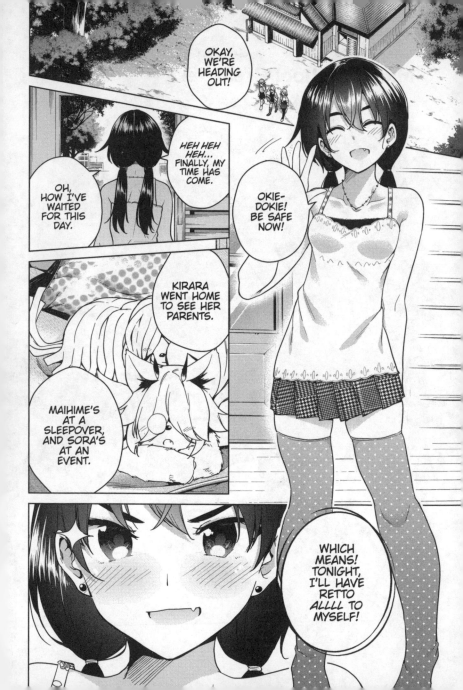

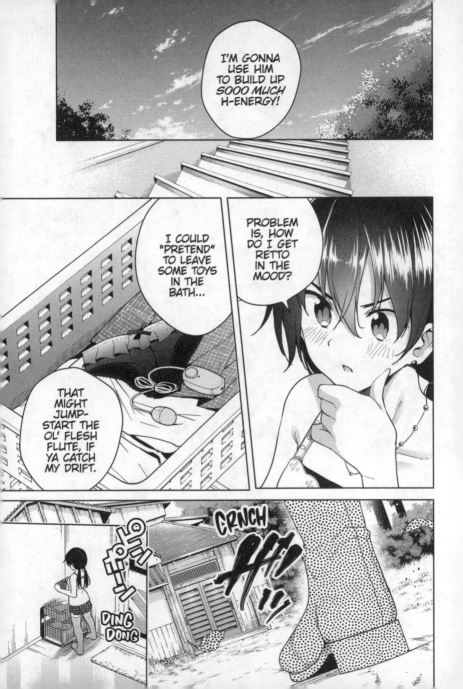

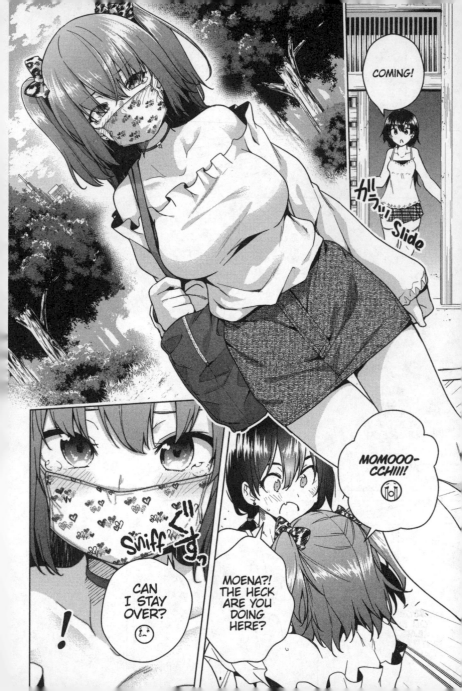

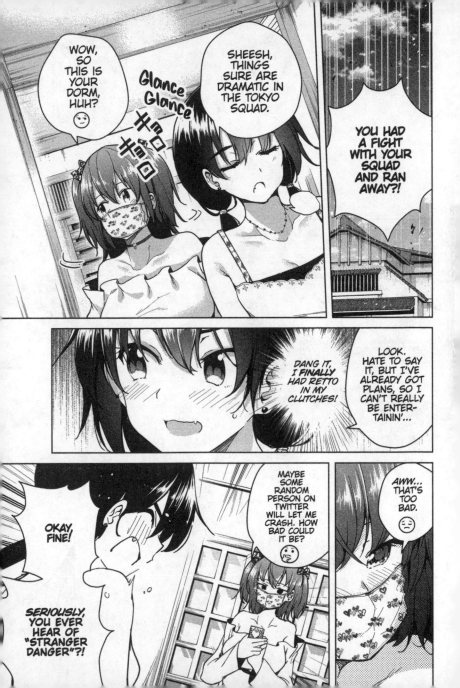

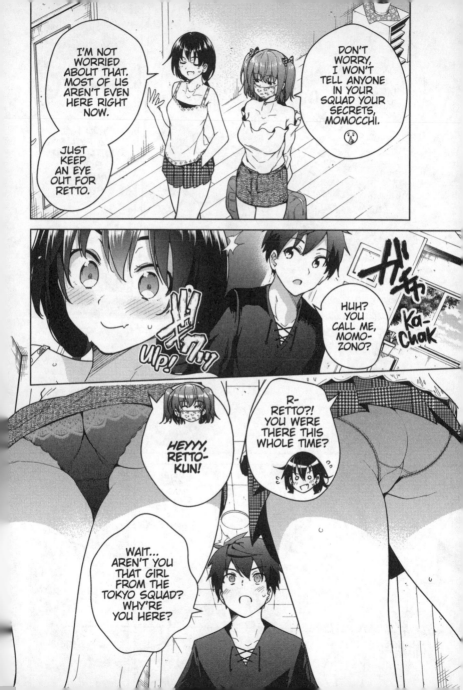

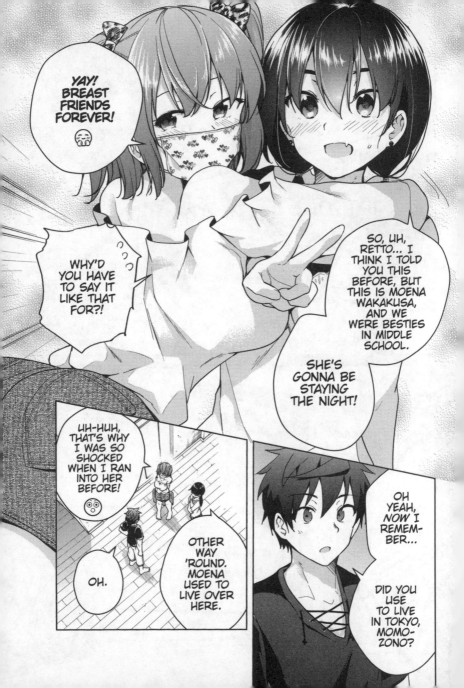

YAY! BREAST FRIENDS FOREVER!

WHY'D YOU HAVE TO SAY IT LIKE THAT FOR?!

SO, UH, RETTO... I THINK I TOLD YOU THIS BEFORE, BUT THIS IS MOENA WAKAKUSA, AND WE WERE BESTIES IN MIDDLE SCHOOL.

SHE'S GONNA BE STAYING THE NIGHT!

UH-HUH, THAT'S WHY I WAS SO SHOCKED WHEN I RAN INTO HER BEFORE!

OTHER WAY 'ROUND. MOENA USED TO LIVE OVER HERE.

OH.

OH YEAH, NOW I REMEM-BER...

DID YOU USE TO LIVE IN TOKYO, MOMO-ZONO?

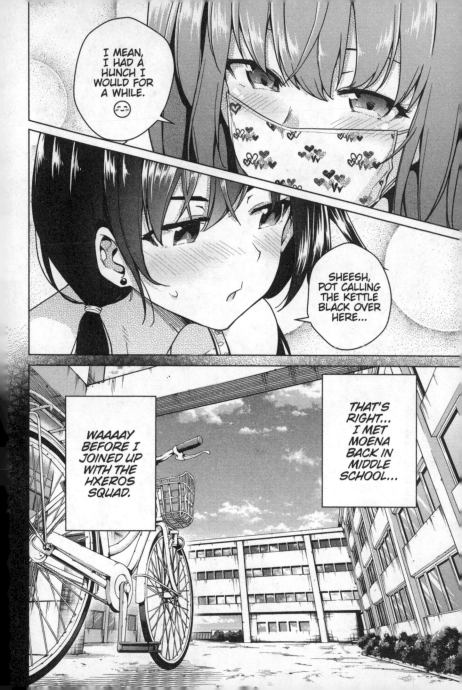

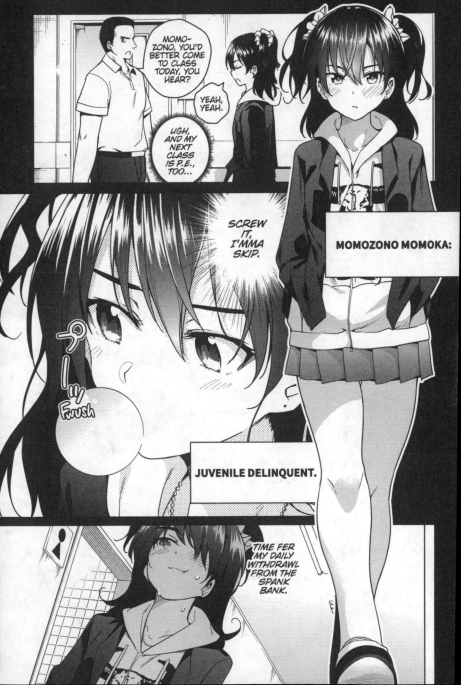

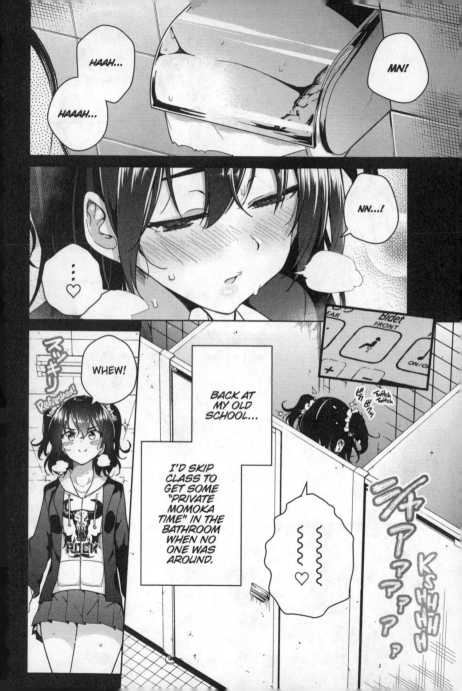

HAAH...

HAAAH...

MN!

NN...!

...♥

WHEW!

リフレッシュ♪

Refreshed!

BACK AT MY OLD SCHOOL...

I'D SKIP CLASS TO GET SOME "PRIVATE MOMOKA TIME" IN THE BATHROOM WHEN NO ONE WAS AROUND.

Bidet
FRONT
REAR
ON/O

Twitch Twitch

♥

〜〜〜

♥

シャアアアアア

KSHHH

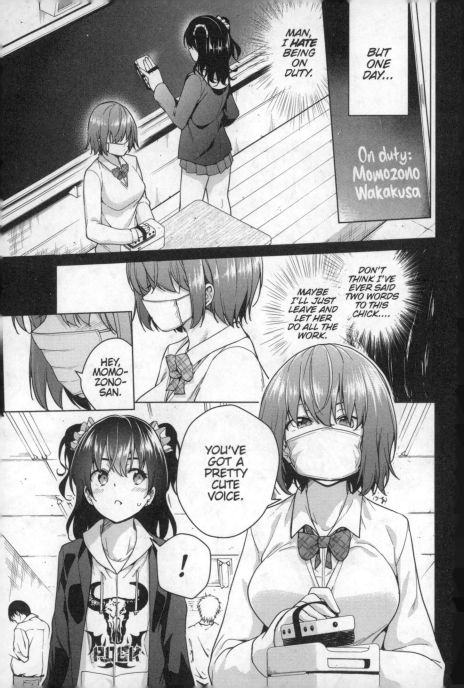

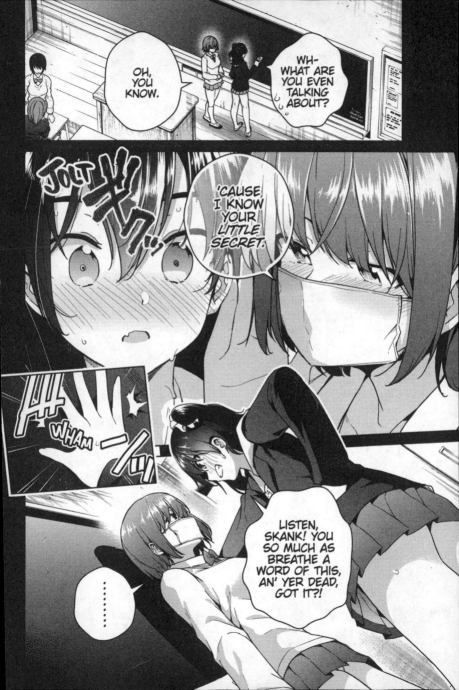

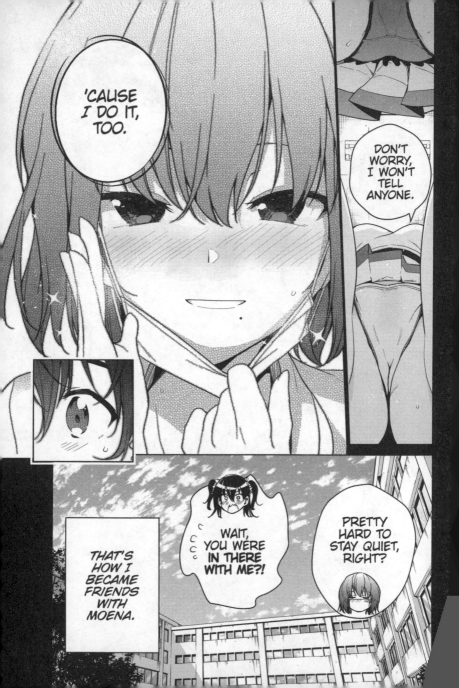

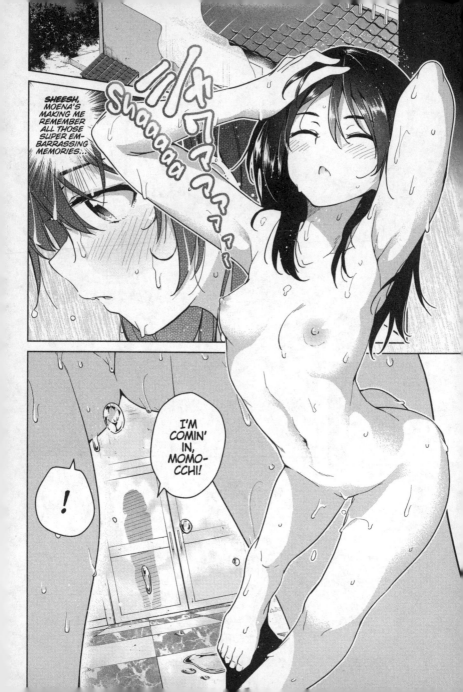

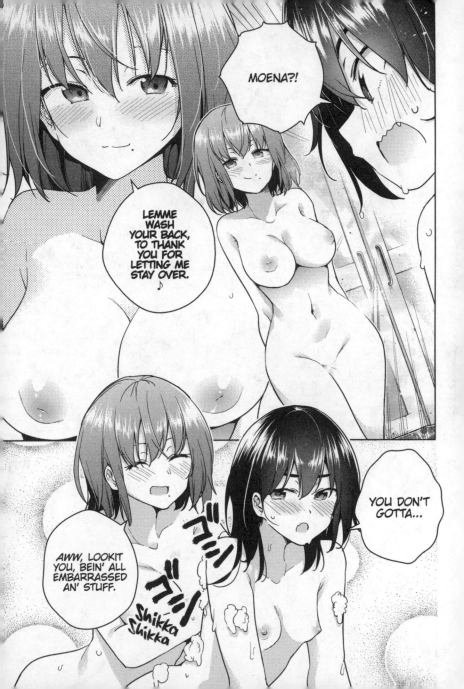

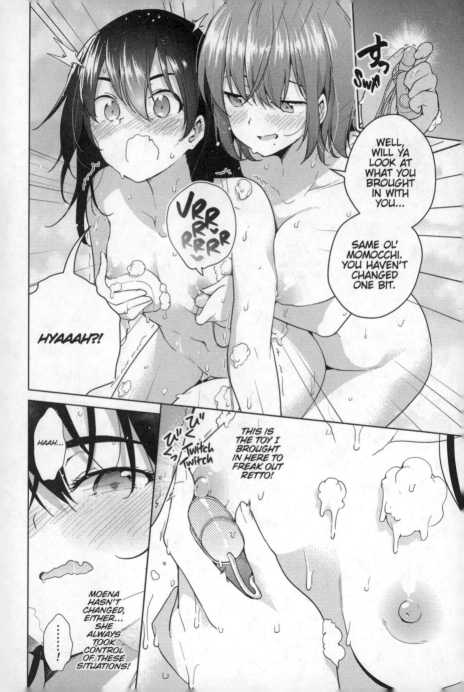

SWA

VRRRRRRR

WELL, WILL YA LOOK AT WHAT YOU BROUGHT IN WITH YOU...

SAME OL' MOMOCCHI. YOU HAVEN'T CHANGED ONE BIT.

HYAAAH?!

HAAH...

Twitch Twitch

THIS IS THE TOY I BROUGHT IN HERE TO FREAK OUT RETTO!

MOENA HASN'T CHANGED, EITHER... SHE ALWAYS TOOK CONTROL OF THESE SITUATIONS!

·····!

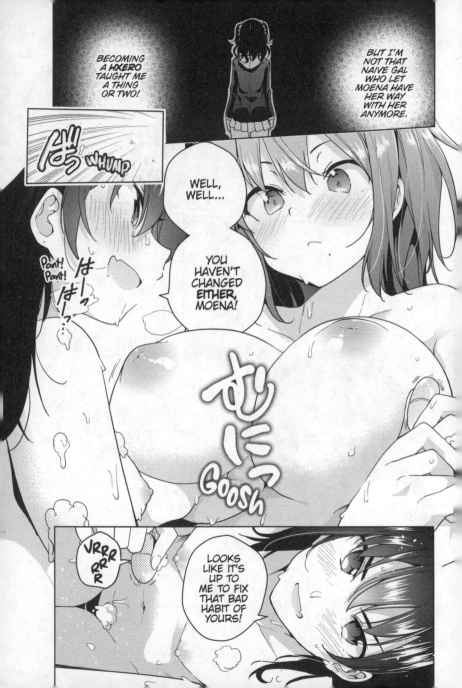

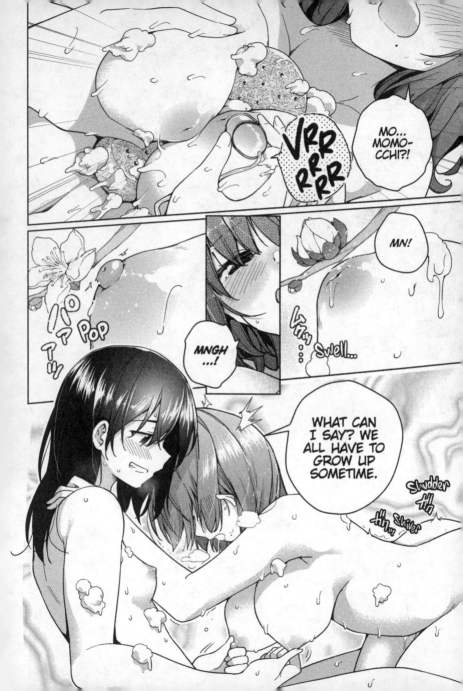

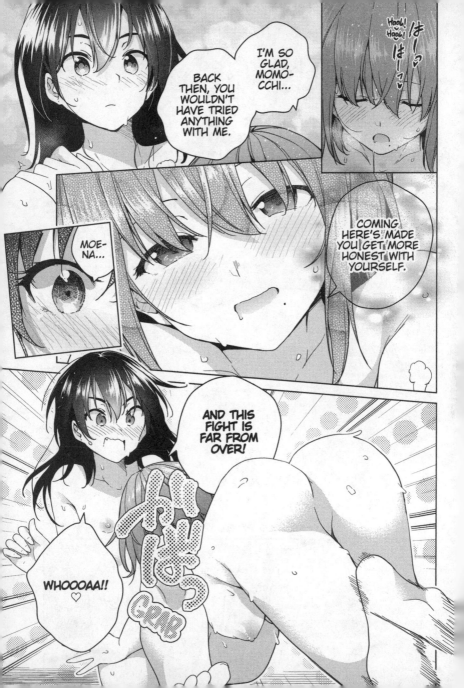

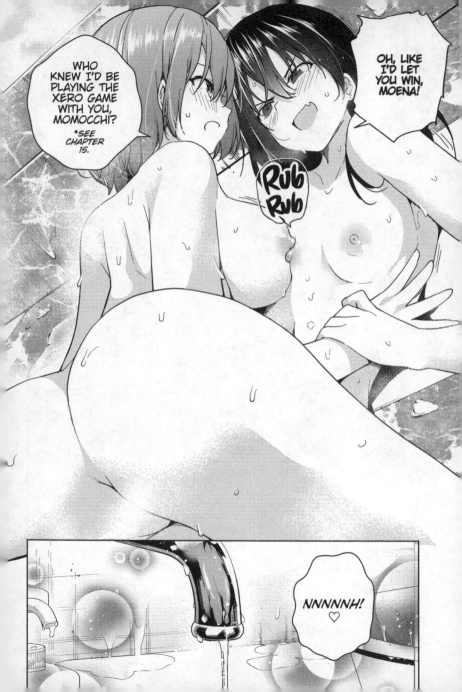

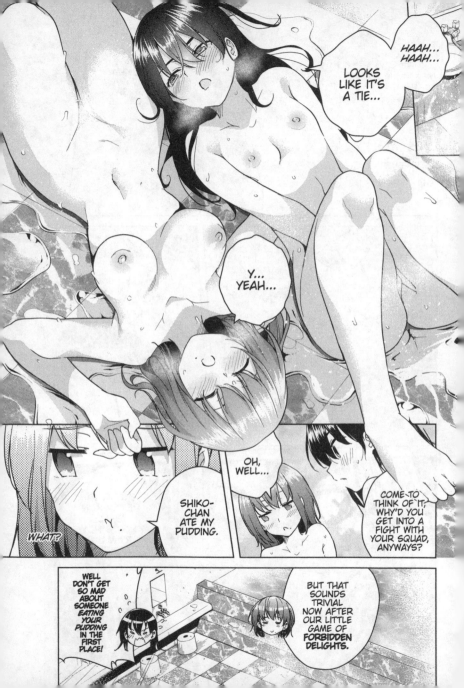

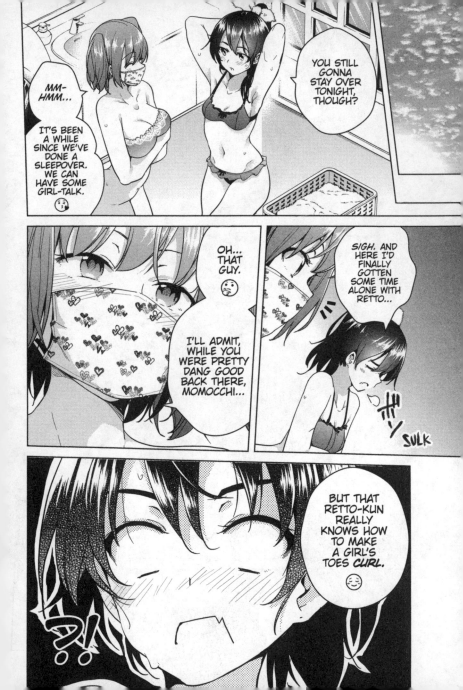

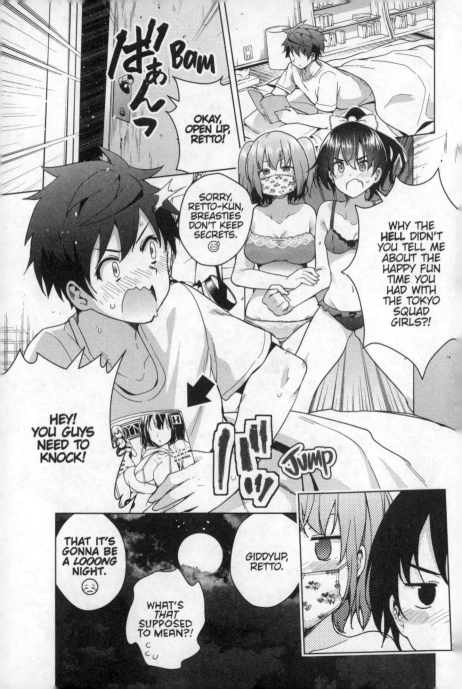

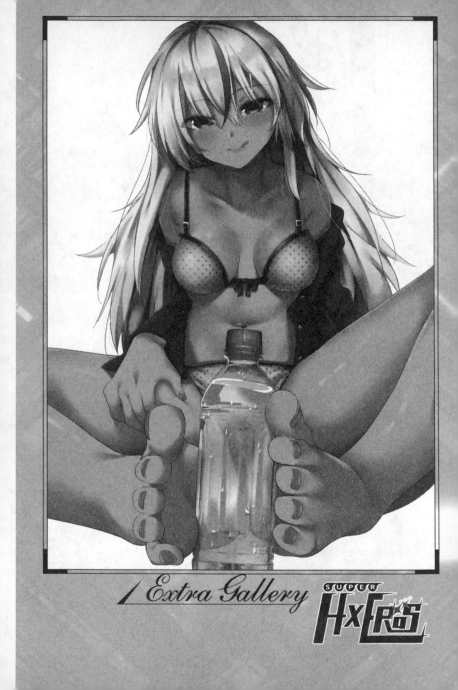

Extra Gallery

SUPER H×EROS

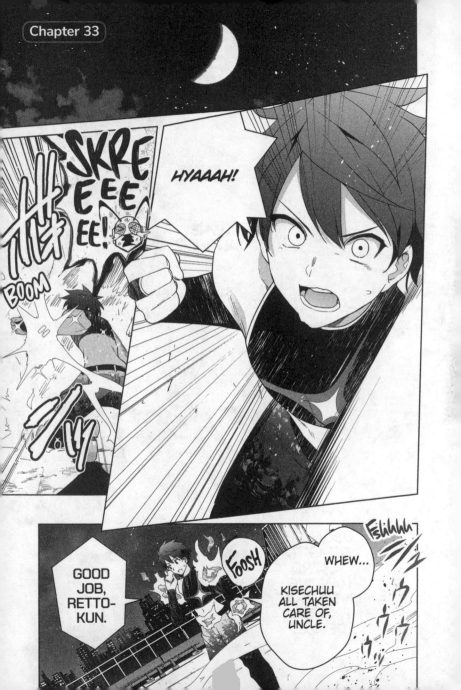

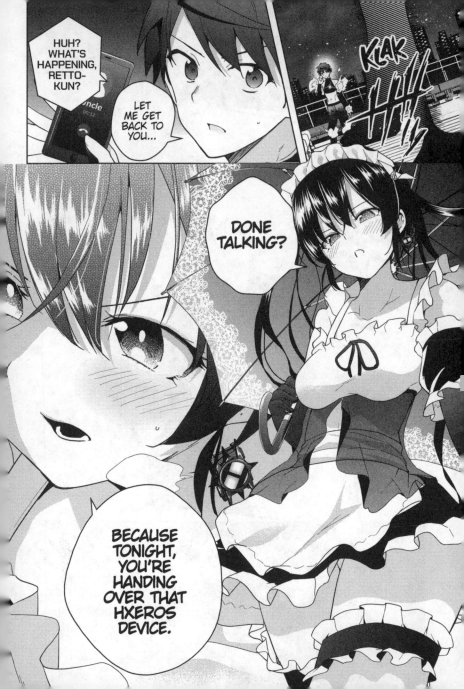

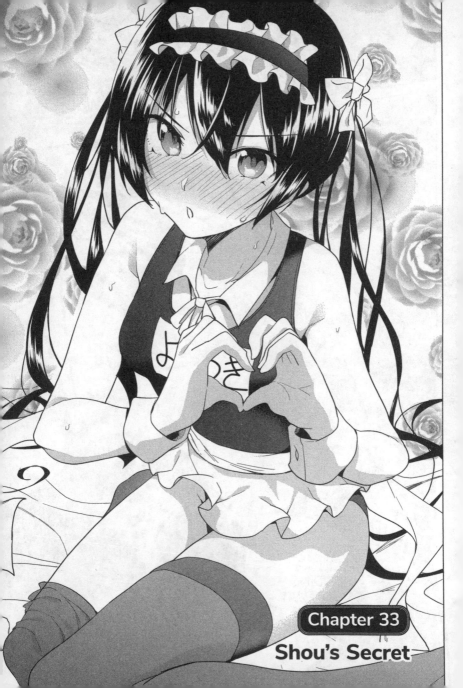

Chapter 33

Shou's Secret

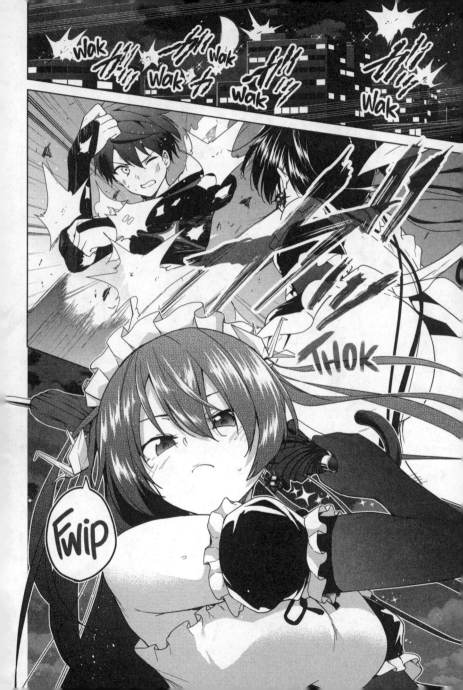

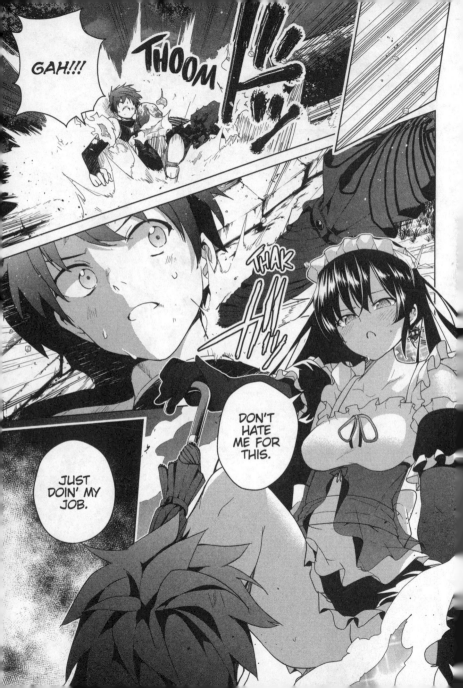

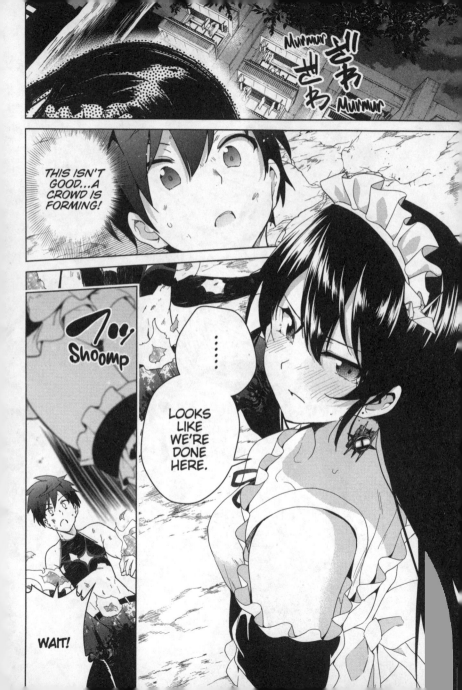

MURMUR
MURMUR
MURMUR

THIS ISN'T GOOD...A CROWD IS FORMING!

SHOOMP

.....

LOOKS LIKE WE'RE DONE HERE.

WAIT!

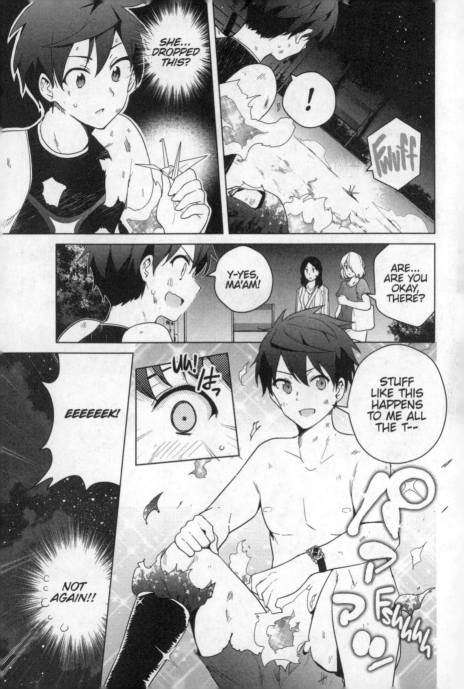

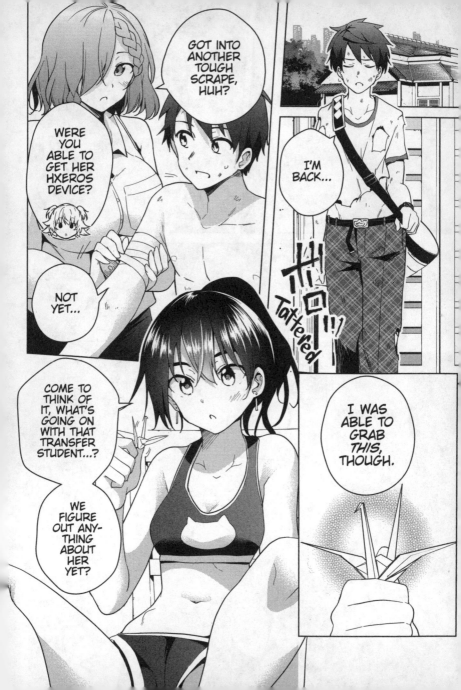

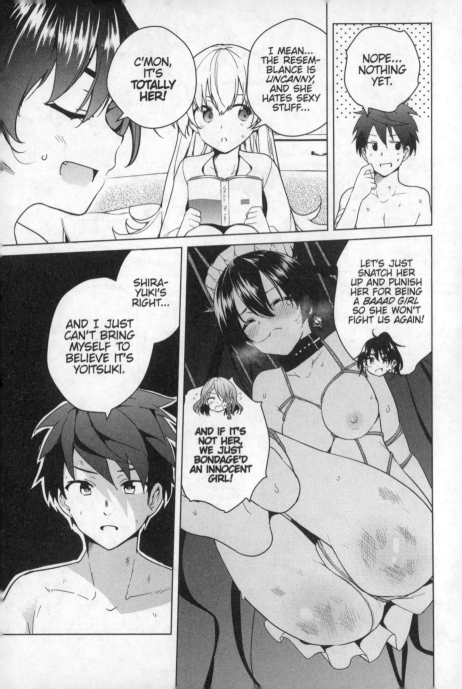

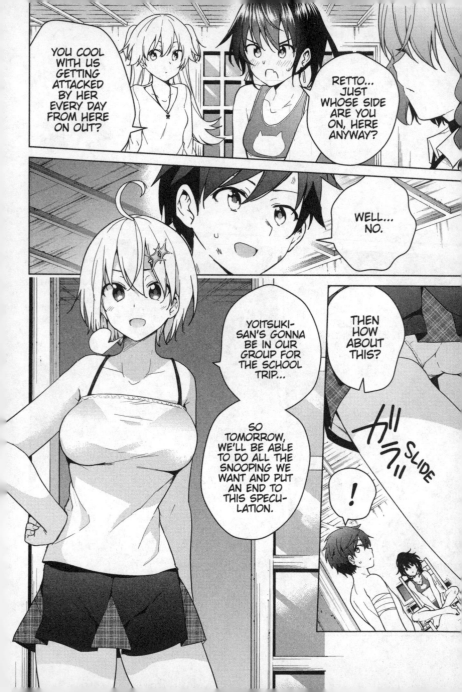

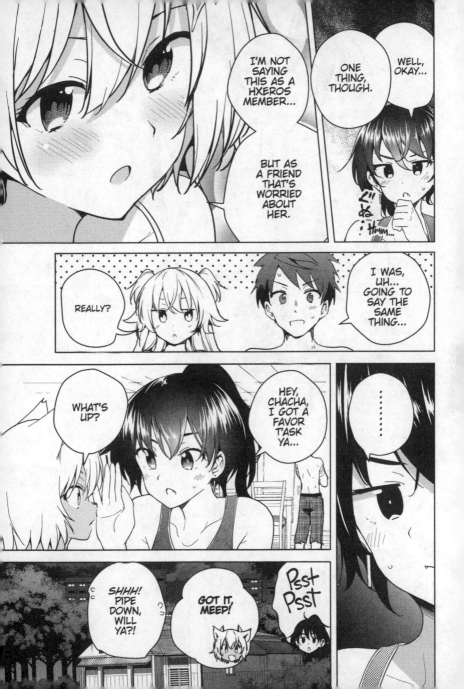

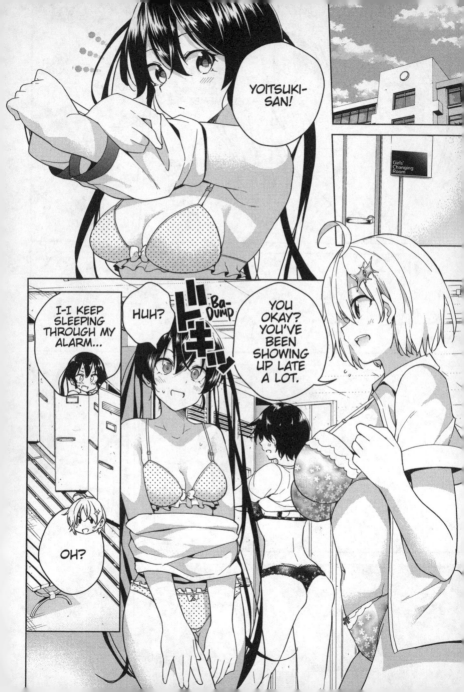

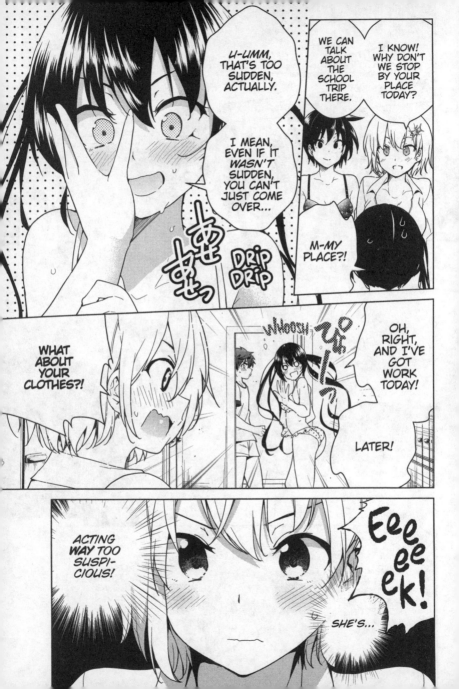

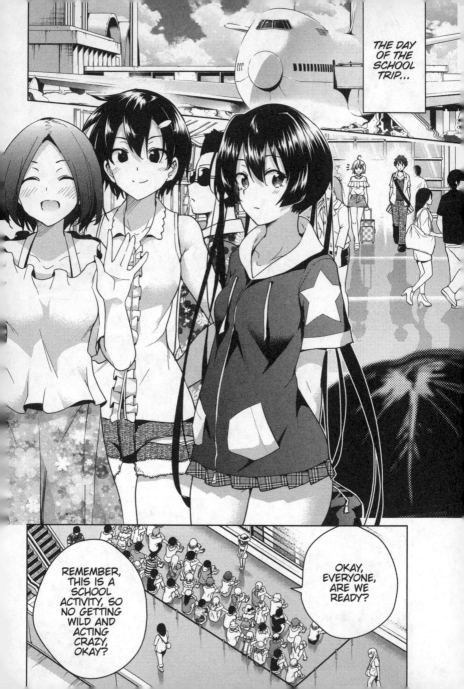

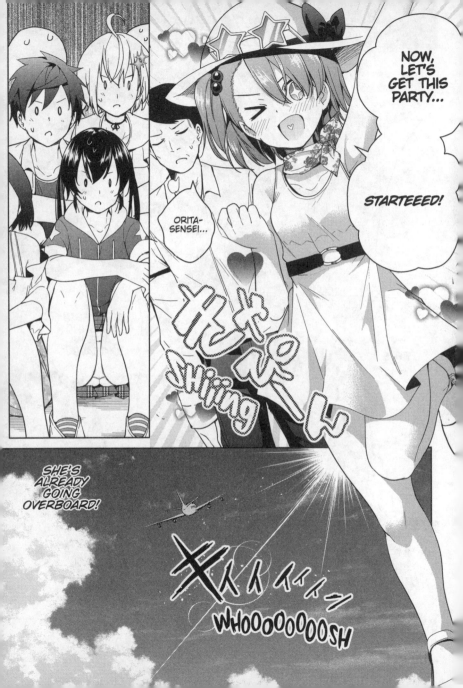

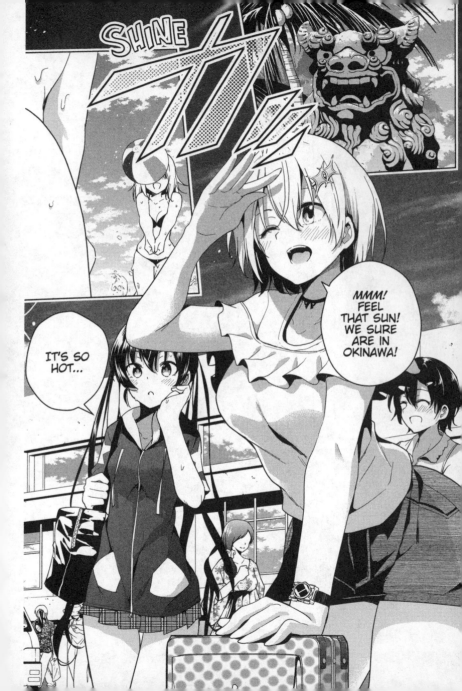

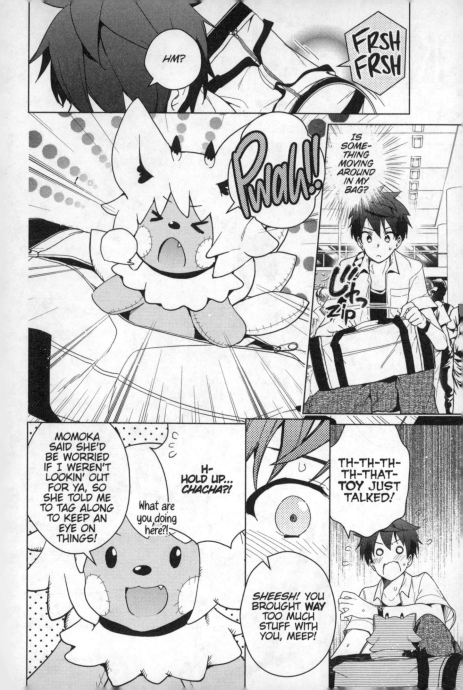

HM?

FRSH FRSH

PWAH!!

IS SOMETHING MOVING AROUND IN MY BAG?

ZIP

MOMOKA SAID SHE'D BE WORRIED IF I WEREN'T LOOKIN' OUT FOR YA, SO SHE TOLD ME TO TAG ALONG TO KEEP AN EYE ON THINGS!

H-HOLD UP... CHACHA?!

What are you doing here?!

TH-TH-TH-TH-THAT TOY JUST TALKED!

SHEESH! YOU BROUGHT WAY TOO MUCH STUFF WITH YOU, MEEP!

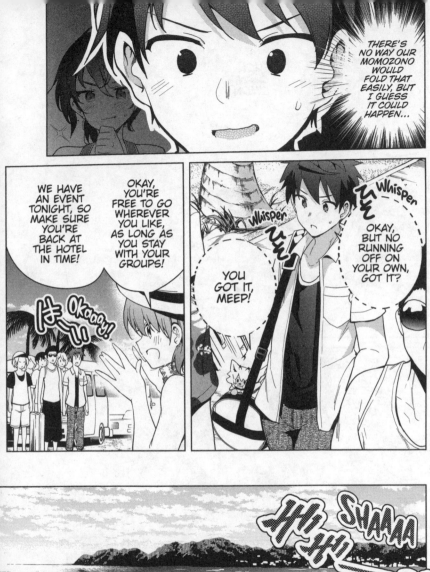

THERE'S NO WAY OUR MOMOZONO WOULD FOLD THAT EASILY, BUT I GUESS IT COULD HAPPEN...

OKAY, YOU'RE FREE TO GO WHEREVER YOU LIKE, AS LONG AS YOU STAY WITH YOUR GROUPS!

WE HAVE AN EVENT TONIGHT, SO MAKE SURE YOU'RE BACK AT THE HOTEL IN TIME!

Okaaay!

OKAY, BUT NO RUNNING OFF ON YOUR OWN, GOT IT?

Whisper

Whisper

YOU GOT IT, MEEP!

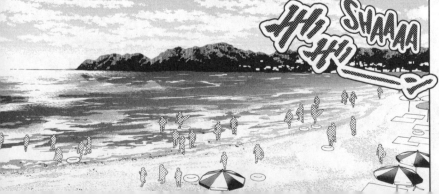

SHAAAA

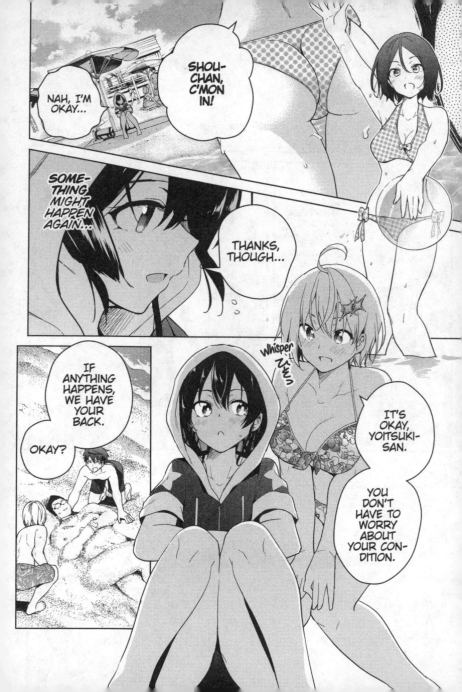

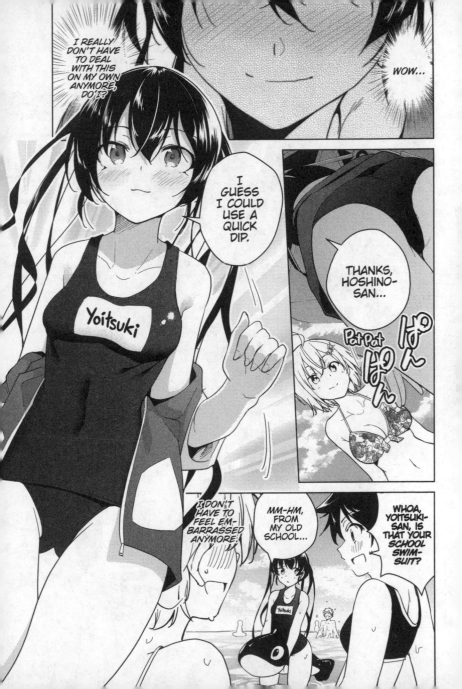

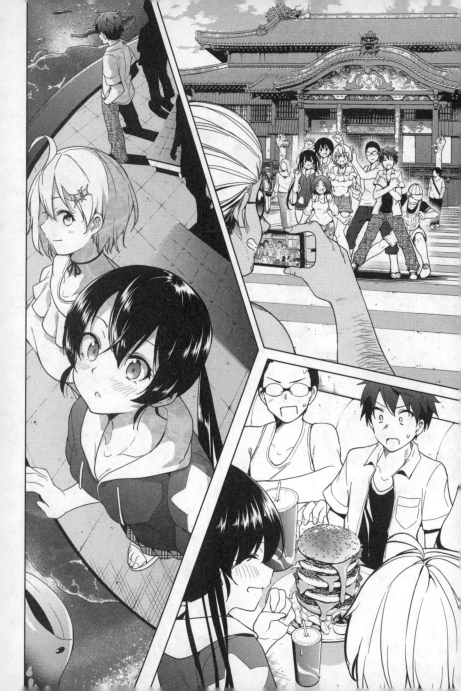

NNH...

LESSEE...
IF I'M REMEMBERING THINGS RIGHT... HUMANS BUILD UP H-HENERGY...

IN PLACES THAT STICK OUT OR CAVE IN!

JOLT

LIKE HERE...

SQUISH SQUISH

IS THIS THE SPOT?

POKE

HWAH?! ♥

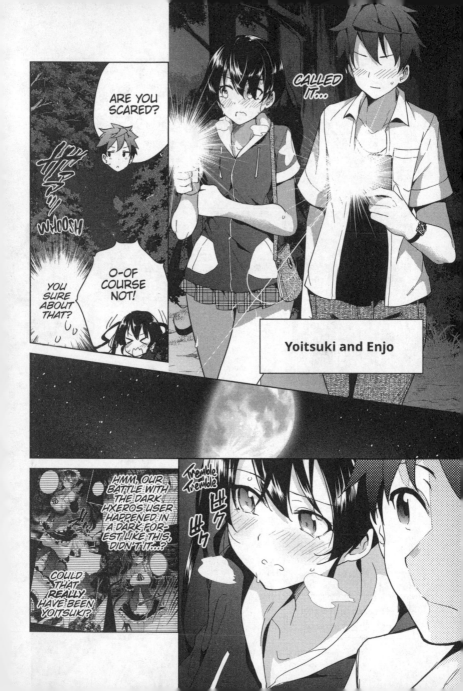

ARE YOU SCARED?

WHOOSH

O-OF COURSE NOT!

YOU SURE ABOUT THAT?

CALLED IT...

Yoitsuki and Enjo

HMM, OUR BATTLE WITH THE DARK HXEROS USER HAPPENED IN A DARK FOREST LIKE THIS, DIDN'T IT...?

COULD THAT REALLY HAVE BEEN YOITSUKI?

Tremble Tremble

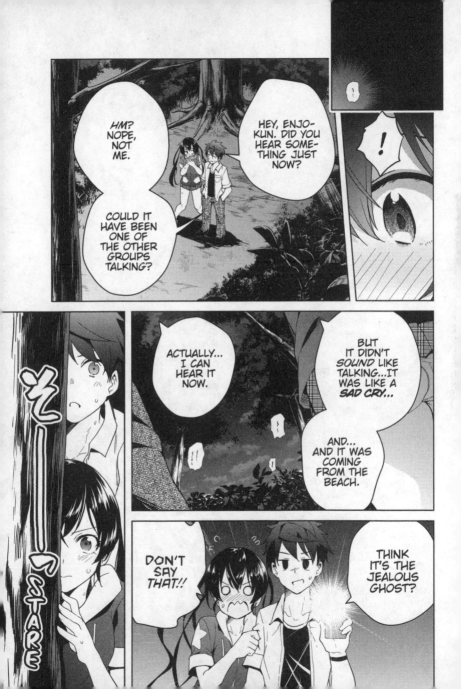

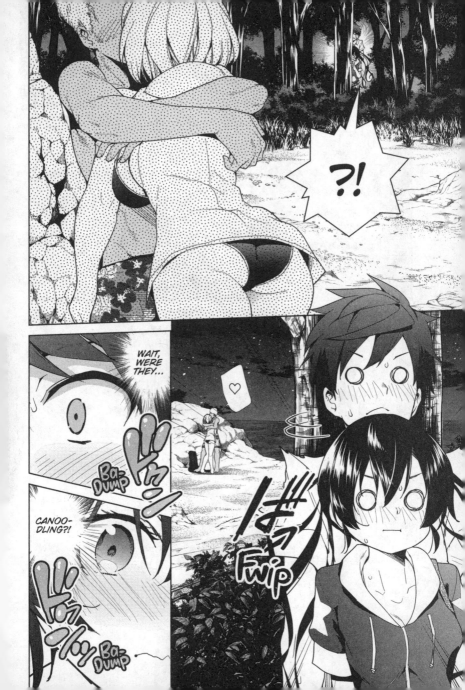

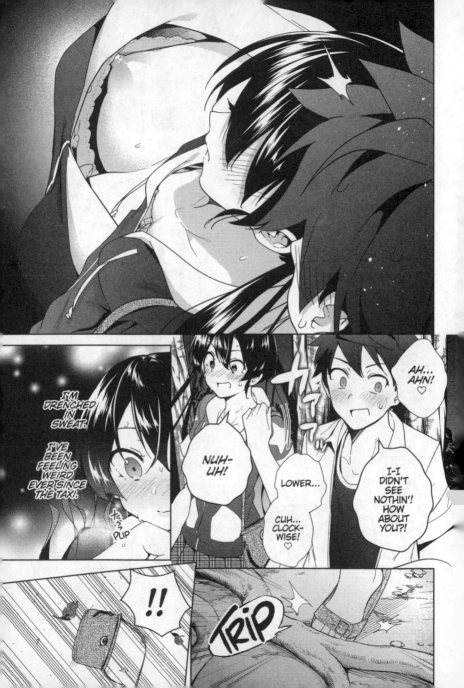

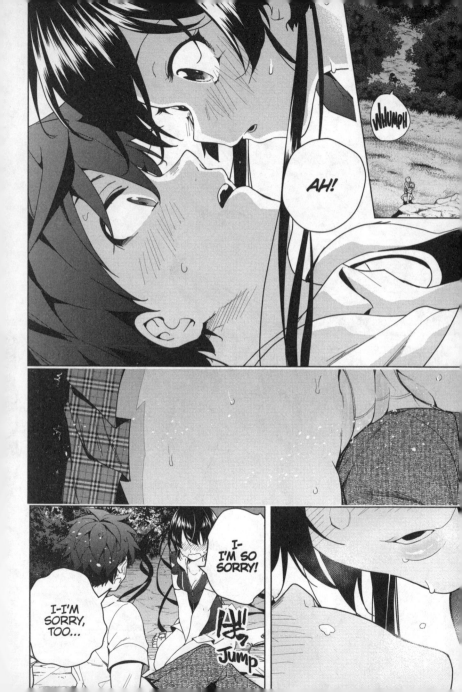

WHUMPH

AH!

I-
I'M SO
SORRY!

I-I'M
SORRY,
TOO...

AH!!
Jump

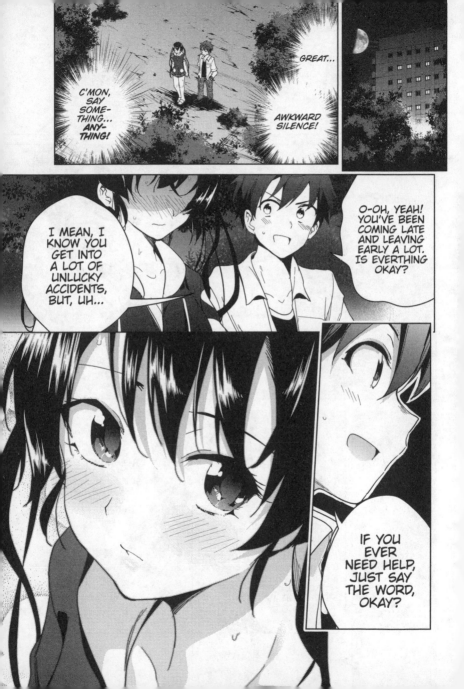

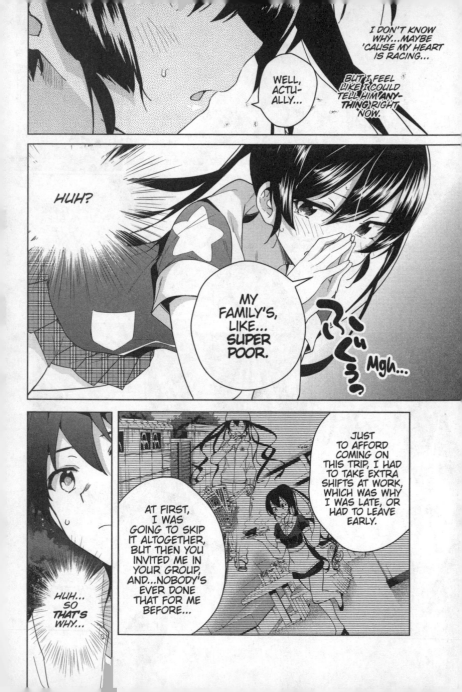

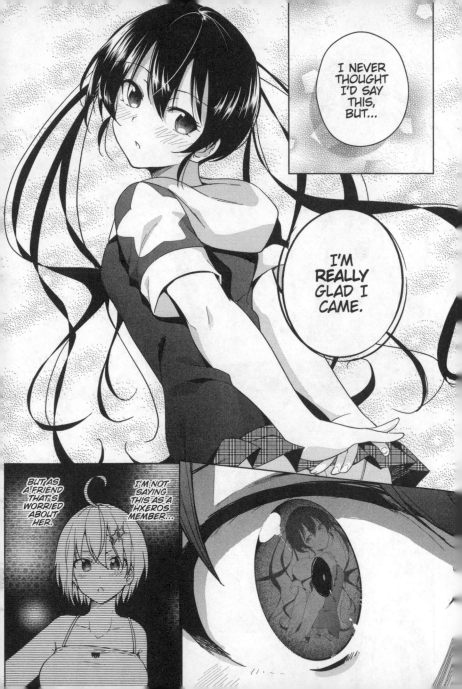

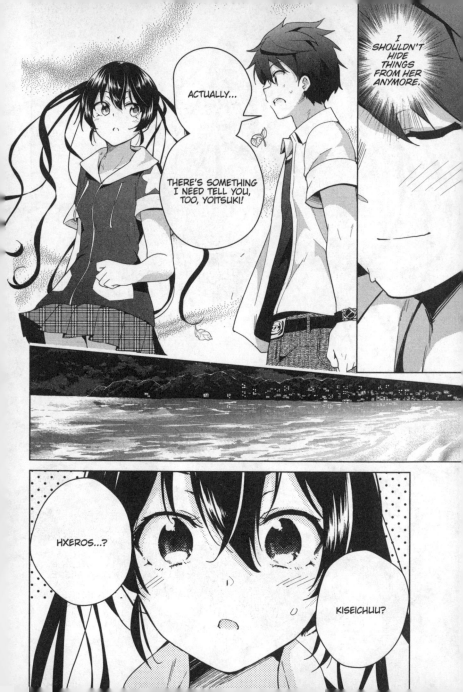

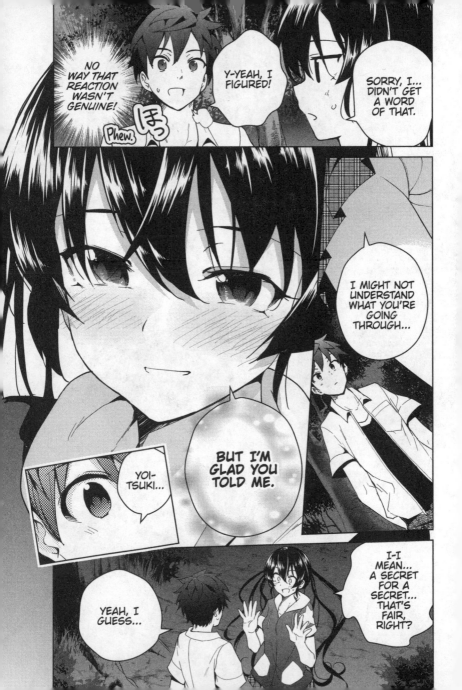

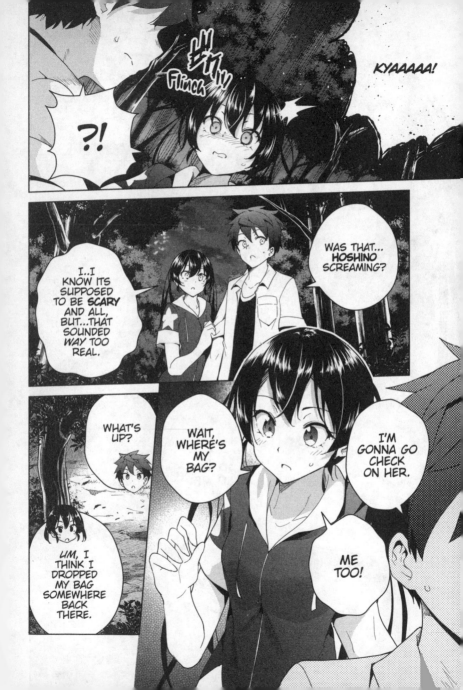